HOME FIRES

A Memoir

by Elaine Cheyney

HOME FIRES: A MEMOIR
Matting Leah Publishing Company/August 2023

Published by Matting Leah Publishing Company
Warwick, New York

Cover Design by Erin Mattingly

Book Design by Kristine Carney

Cheyney, Elaine, author.
Home fires : a memoir / by Elaine Cheyney.
Warwick, New York : Matting Leah Publishing Company, [2023]
ISBN: 978-0-9905764-5-7 (paperback)
LCSH: Cheyney, Elaine. | Jewish women--England--20th century--Biography. |

Autobiography --Jewish authors. | World War, 1939-1945--England--Personal narratives. | War brides-- United States--Biography. | Divorced women--United States--Biography. | Single mothers-- United States--Biography. | Antisemitism--Personal narratives. | LCGFT: Autobiographies. | BISAC: BIOGRAPHY & AUTOBIOGRAPHY / Jewish. | BIOGRAPHY & AUTOBIOGRAPHY / Women. | HISTORY / Europe / Great Britain / 20th Century. | FAMILY & RELATIONSHIPS / Divorce & Separation.
Classification: LCC: HQ1172 .C54 2023 | DDC: 305.48/8924--dc23

For Ivor, Gloria, and Brian.

I don't think of all the misery
but of the beauty that still remains.
- Anne Frank

PART I

THE EARLIEST MEMORY

I sat cheerfully in the pram with my one-year-old sister, Gloria, in our matching white bonnets. It was an usually mild and splendid day in May, 1937. With Mum's supervision, our big brother, Ivor, pushed the pram towards the grand procession. Our London neighborhood streets overflowed with festivity. At just three-years-old, I felt the excitement surrounding me as the King of England was about to be crowned. The coronation of King George VI was a celebration of the ages. The opulent procession towards Buckingham Palace was most extravagant. This is my earliest recollection.

I was a young child and experienced only the merriment, energy, and pageantry of the royal event. I was unaware of how King George VI ascended the throne. His older brother, Edward VIII was king. King Edward abdicated the throne to marry Wallis Simpson, a socialite from the United States. Her divorced status was a threat to the monarchy. Their union was a scandal throughout Great Britain. It was controversial and did not align with being the nominal head of the Church of England. The royal family disagreed with Edward's leanings toward right wing authoritarianism. Edward and Mrs. Simpson consorted with Hitler and were suspected of having Nazi connections. Had Edward remained on the throne during World War II, which would begin two years hence, the results for England may well have been disastrous.

I was not aware of family rifts, divorce, war, or a country called the United States. At three-years-old I had no idea that life would be anything other than one long and festive parade.

ROSALEE

At that early age, I already viewed my Mum, Rosalee, as a stunningly beautiful, kind-hearted, and compassionate woman. I thought her existence to be effervescent and effortless. I later learned that beautiful Rosalee suffered great losses and heartache as a young girl growing up in the East End of London. Nobody is immune to misfortune in life.

When Mum and her sister, Jenny, were teenagers, their mother died of cancer at only 45-years-old. My callous grandfather brought his girlfriend to the funeral and introduced her to Rosalee and Jenny as their new mother. Only months after the funeral, my grandfather and his new wife made plans to send my Mum to the United States to live with cousins in New Jersey. My Mum was 18-years-old and had her passport and papers to leave. One last vacation to the Isle of Wight was arranged with her dearest childhood friends as a special way to say farewell. While on holiday, my Mum met and fell in love with my father, Al Cheyney. What a gorgeous couple they made. Both lived in the East End of London. Although they lived only blocks apart, the two had never met. Shortly thereafter, Al proposed. My Mum accepted and did not go to America at that juncture.

My heart ached for Mum as I recognized the deep sadness in her life as his wife. She was a servant to Dad and memories of his verbal abuse towards her has always remained with me. I found it astonishing that their first seven years together were filled with happiness. I never understood what changes took place after such happiness that created the dysfunctional relationship that remained between them. He was demeaning towards my three siblings, Ivor, Gloria and Brian. My heart would break when he belittled them, yet he treated me with love in their presence. It was as if he only had room in his heart to love me.

AL

When World War II started in 1939, Dad was drafted into the Royal Air Force (RAF). While the airmen were in line giving their personal information, Dad heard the guys in front of him answer when each was asked what their religion was. One replied "C of E" (Church of England), and another answered "R.C." for Roman Catholic. When it was Dad's turn, he playfully spelled out "J-E-W."

The RAF stationed Dad at British bases during the early years of the war until 1942, when he was sent to Lahore, India. He was an airplane mechanic for the bombers that came in from reconnaissance flights. The plane he worked on was an American, two-engine bomber called a B-26 Marauder, known commonly as *Widowmaker*. Painted across the plane by the pilots and crew was its nickname, *The Flying Prostitute*. The catchy name was apparently because it was a fast plane with small wings and had no visible means of support. When Dad was not fixing engines, he enjoyed his downtime. On occasion, the airmen put on shows for their own regiment. A tailor by trade, Dad was involved with the scene building, costume making, and whatever else it took to put on a good and entertaining show. He also started a hiking group with the local Indian boys. He had appreciated his time with the British Boy Scouts as a young lad and wanted to pass on that experience. One of his many hiking trips with the Indian boys included a climb up the Lower Himalayas. Dad enjoyed his time in India and always held the Indian people in high regard. Not too long after World War II, India split into two countries, India and Pakistan, and the region became more war-torn than when Dad was stationed there in the Royal Air Force.

OPERATION PIED PIPER

Back at home, things had changed dramatically during the war years for my family. Air raid drills were conducted at school. Children were given instructions in regard to properly using gas masks and to dive under our desks for protection from flying objects if there was a raid. It was just another game for us as we had no idea what was really going on. Soon the war began to heat up in London.

My brother, Ivor, was eight-years-old and I was five when we were evacuated to the countryside in order to escape the London Blitz. My sister, Gloria, was only four and deemed too young by the government to be sent away from Mum. Our youngest brother, Brian was not yet born. On September 1, 1939, two days before Britain and France declared war on Nazi Germany, Mum took us to the railway station where hundreds of other children were lined up. Each child packed a gas mask and small bag of personal items. We were loaded on trains like cattle and sent off to places unknown to us. This was not an adventure by any means. Instead, we were tearfully torn apart from our loving families. There was heartache wherever you looked. Each parent said mournful goodbyes to their children for they were only too aware if, or when, they would see each other again. Seeing adults and children alike in such misery was distressing. There was indescribable sorrow. The fear was palpable.

When we arrived at a train station at the end of our trip, we were lined up by age and separated into groups of girls and boys. We stayed in line until a family came along and picked one or two children to take home with them. If they were farmers, they were more likely to pick older, stronger boys who could work on their farms. Some families picked children because they matched the ages of their own children and might be good companions for them. For me, being separated from my big brother, Ivor, was the worst that could happen. Alas, it did.

I was chosen by an older childless couple. The Victorian way in which they cared for me was kind but outdated. They had no hands-on experience raising a child and I was their guinea pig. They believed that a child must use the potty at least once a day. They would remove the China pot from under the bed and place it in the middle of the kitchen. I was told I must sit on the hard porcelain pot until I did what was expected. My body did not respond well to this method and, sometimes, I was made to sit there for hours until they were satisfied. I had a ring around my bum for ages.

After leaving this household, both Ivor and I were sent to St. Albans in Hertfordshire, but each to a different family. Ivor was my idol and to know he was nearby was the only bright spot in my young life. The family who took me in were indifferent towards all the children they housed. They taunted me and refused permission for me to visit my brother who was so near. It was never allowed, no matter how much I cried and begged. My host family adamantly forbade me and seemed to enjoy my pain. The great highlight of my days was going to school and watching my brother through the fence. I could see him playing with the bigger children or catch a glimpse of him in classes. One day, I ran across the road in great haste to see him through a playground gate just as a car came along and ran into me. Fortunately, I only received bruises and scratches, but nothing more serious. However, there was so much fuss from the people who saw me knocked to the ground that I didn't get to say hello to my brother after all. What hurt most was to be separated from Ivor.

St. Albans was close enough to London that we could see the skies, red with flames, after the bombing raids by the Germans. Everyone would go out onto their doorsteps to watch the spectacle. It seemed like it meant little to those who safely resided in this little town. It sent the worst kind of fear and anxiety through me, and others like me. I imagined my mother and siblings in London being burned alive. I was overwhelmed with these terrifying thoughts until they came down on the train once again and I saw that they were safe.

About once a month, Mum came on the train from London with my sister Gloria and my baby brother, Brian, who was born shortly before Dad left for India in 1942. I was in awe of my new baby brother. He was in a pram which had a board in the bottom under the mattress that, when lifted, would reveal a place to store needed items for the baby. I was so excited and wanted to push the pram down the street as I played "mummy" with him. The handles were above my head, and I could not see over them. Consequently, I ran into a lamppost and baby Brian slid under the board in the bottom of the pram and out of sight. I could not find him and went into hysterics thinking I had lost him. Fortunately, Mum was close at hand and pulled Brian out from under the lid in the bottom of the pram like a magician. She lovingly assured me that he was perfectly all right.

It was always difficult when my mother and siblings left and returned to London. The devastation I experienced while I was away from them was so terrible that I was barely able to function. The situation felt more cruel because I had been evacuated to a family who were nearly negligent with their childcare. Love and empathy was never present. I was evolving into a depressed young girl.

The family was given a small stipend for each child they housed. Money was their incentive rather than kindness, so they took in far too many children. We slept four to a single bed, two at the head and two at the toe. Each of us got a terrible case of head lice. There was little my mother could do during her visits to help. She applied kerosene to my scalp to kill the parasites. Her tears of distress mingled with the noxious fumes. She gently picked through my hair to comb the lice out one by one. I felt her deep love for me which was the best medicine.

Still marked with a ring around my bum from the previous home, this new family was horribly strict about using the toilet. The bathroom was in the backyard. It was similar to an outhouse but had the addition of a chain to flush the toilet. They refused to let us use the toilet after we had been sent to bed early in the evening. They enforced this by locking the back door. Most families kept a pot under the bed. That was not permitted here because they didn't want to empty our pots the next day. As I couldn't use the toilet at night, I was quite afraid of wetting the bed. This contributed to my deepening depression.

In addition to such stressful housing conditions, there was another great threat to the area where we lived. German planes could not land back in Germany with loaded bombs on board, so they would drop the last of their ammunition wherever they happened to fly after their raids. St. Albans was on many occasions along their flight path out of England. This concerned my parents greatly. This area was too close to London to be a safe haven for children.

Once again, off we went into the countryside in search of a safer place to live further away from London. Mum's sister and her two children evacuated to the beautiful little village of South Petherton in Somerset. When my Aunt Jenny heard of our predicament, she found the most wonderful family for me, the Gentles, a mile up the road from her. By that time, Gloria was old enough also to be evacuated, and my aunt discovered another good family for her only doors away from me. The countryside of Somerset was about 150 miles away from our London home. Mum decided Ivor would be more helpful at home, so he did not join the evacuees this time, but went back to London with her and baby Brian.

There was a completely different feeling for me in Somerset. Mr. & Mrs. Gentle, so true to their name, were kindness itself. I was seven by then, and one of their daughters, Pam, was just my age, while another daughter, Beryl, was a few years younger. Their oldest was sixteen and, shortly after I arrived, she was engaged to marry. The whole family was caring and understanding, and I came to love them all dearly.

Their tiny home felt like a dollhouse to me. Mrs. Gentle had a sewing machine in the living room where she would sit all day and sew leather gloves. A company would drop off batches of unsewn gloves to each home in the countryside and the ladies were paid for each batch they could sew. This was one of the few ways the country women could contribute towards the income of their families. There were no factories near their little town and the men mostly farmed or were in the service.

Mr. Gentle was a sweet man. He served in the British Army in the First World War and was still recovering from injuries. He adopted a monkey, a macaque named Mr. Tibbles, which had belonged to a fellow soldier who was killed in the war. Apparently, the clever monkey was taught how to steal cigarettes from other soldiers. Mr. Gentle boasted, thanks to Mr. Tibbles, he was never in want of a smoke. We loved his stories about the mischievous little primate. We found solace in the laughter.

My little sister, Gloria, was housed just down the street with a good family that had three adult daughters and a son. Auntie Olive, as we affectionately called the mother, was wonderful to take on another child. While with her new caretakers, Gloria got a dreadful rash all over her body. She was taken to a clinic daily for scalding hot baths. As I was the big sister, I could not let her go through the misery alone, so I joined her on each visit. When she cried because the water was burning her tender skin, I asked to be put in the bath with her as though I could possibly absorb her pain.

It eased our sorrows greatly to have my aunt and cousins close by and we passed them on our way to school. Despite that, I still felt homesick for my family and never became a playful child. I felt deeply depressed and unable to quell my sadness.

There were times when, in my loneliness, I would go out to the fields near the house. Over the wire fence, I could see workers as they picked potatoes and apples. I did not know that they were Italian and German prisoners of war. They came up to the fence and tried to chat with me. Although language was a barrier, there was such great longing in their faces as they tried to tell me about their own families. They would hastily retrieve little black and white pictures of their children from inner pockets to share with me. They suffered such sadness not knowing what was happening to their families so far away. Even as a child, I strongly sensed their loneliness and sorrow. I smiled at them and touched their faces to try to cheer them up. I would feel a stray tear fall on my cheek on many occasions. My young heart ached for them. The prisoners often gifted me with an apple. It was all they had to give, although their kind smiles had been enough for me. These tender moments of connection were as heartwarming as they were heart-wrenching. We endured the same war on different sides of a fence that neither had constructed.

14

While in Somerset, there were times when the bombing would cease and a great sense of hope would come to the weary Londoners. My Mum would take the train with Ivor and Brian and pick up Gloria and me to take us back to London. These were the happiest days for us and we were overjoyed to be together. Unknowingly, we were in even greater danger traveling on trains than sitting in our own living rooms. The Germans strategically bombed railways to destroy England's ability to transport goods and troops. Even if I had known the risk, I believed that to die together was better than to live apart.

While home in London, the Blitz started again at full throttle. Mum rushed us to the back garden into the tiny bomb shelter. It held a few blankets and pillows and a mattress that fit wall-to-wall. The shelter could not protect us from a direct hit by a bomb, but it could protect us from flying shrapnel. We would sit and watch through a crack in the shelter door as the skies were alive with German fighters battling with our RAF boys. The thunderous bangs, the blazing light flashes and the smokey scent will forever be ingrained in my being.

Barrage balloons floated overhead. These balloons floated at different heights and were tethered by ropes to the ground at a local children's park. They looked like replicas of the Hindenburg without the passengers. Their purpose was to tangle the German planes. If aircraft flew too low, they would find themselves in a net of barrage balloons. The searchlights were about a half mile from our backyard, and they would beam onto the German planes. We could hear the ack-ack-ack of the anti-aircraft guns very close-by. Our boys shot at the German bombers. The British soldiers tried to destroy the bombers before they could do more damage. One German pilot went down in the school playing field close to our house and was taken prisoner. It was all so terribly frightening. Fear filled children and adults alike.

Germans occupied Guernsey and Jersey Islands, which were so close to England that there was great fear that Hitler could get through to the British Isles too. While bomb raids continued, the Axis powers agreed that certain major historical monuments like St. Paul's Cathedral, Big Ben, the Houses of Parliament, and Buckingham Palace were not to be destroyed. Hitler wanted these and many others throughout Great Britain when he, presumably, won the war.

Despite these proclamations, precision bombing by either side was lacking. It was absurd to guarantee to save these high-profile locations. Weather conditions and blackouts made it difficult to find intended targets such as ammunition factories, shipyards, and railroads. Unsurprisingly, St. Paul's Cathedral was hit and was stopped from burning down only due to the quick reactions of fire crews and volunteers. Buckingham Palace was hit a number of times because of mechanical issues and poor visibility. On account of all this, after nightfall, it was paramount that our homes were completely darkened, with no light appearing anywhere at all.

There were times when the siren would sound to alert us to get to the shelters, but the bombs would start to drop before we could get to the back door. During those raids, Mum quickly put us all under the staircase, which could have protected us if the house went down around us. Gloria and I cried when we were put under the stairs because mice had been spotted there and we were terrified. As children, the mice seemed more of a threat to us than a bomb.

Houses all around us were bombed to the ground during those long war years, yet ours, our Auntie Anne's, and some neighbors' houses were spared. On one occasion, the blast of a nearby bomb broke some of our windows. My uncle was a warden and regularly went out to look for people who were buried under the rubble. Although Mum was not officially a warden, she often shared in these search duties. When raids ceased again for a brief time, Mum would rush us back to the safety of Somerset.

Somehow, we always found moments of laughter. Humor had a beautiful way of bonding us together while giving us some small sense of relief. On one occasion, an old Jewish man went to use the outhouse moments before a bomb was dropped nearby. When the wardens found the man under the rubble, he was laughing hysterically. He exclaimed, "I pulled the chain to flush and the whole caboodle came down on top of me!"

WOMEN ON THE HOME FRONT

There was much work left for the women of England once the young men had gone to war. Many worked in factories doing what was called "Peace Work." "Land Girls" was the term used for the women who went out to the country to do farm work, which was critical to help feed the British people. Women were expected to "keep the home fires burning" as the sayings and songs told us," 'til the boys come home". The roles of women were transformed from housewives and mothers to factory and farm workers.

Petrol and food were rationed. Each person had a ration book containing coupons. When coupons were used up for the month, that was it. There was a black market for those who could afford to pay a fortune for extra food, although it was frowned upon by the government. It was considered unpatriotic amongst other things, but when people wanted to have a cake for some special occasion, they needed to barter for extra sugar from the grocery store. If you were in a real bind, you did your best to manage or looked to friends and family for help.

At one point, Mum's shoes had worn down to nothing but cardboard and string to hold what was left of her shoes in place. She took buses to get to her father's house and met her stepmother at their front door. Mum showed her the tattered shoes she wore and asked if she could borrow money to buy some second-hand ones. Mum's stepmother flatly refused her, so Mum went home empty-handed and deflated. I passionately believe if my grandfather had answered the door, he would have offered money to Mum, but he was at work in his clothing factory at the time.

Even as a baby, my grandfather's wife left a terrible impression on me. I was quite a chubby baby, and she would pick me up and pretend to love and kiss me. The reality was that she would bite my legs extremely hard and subsequently I would cry for hours. My parents noticed the deep red bite marks on my legs and agreed we would never return for a visit again.

YANKS

Shortly after the Pearl Harbor bombings by the Japanese in 1942, American soldiers and airmen arrived in England. They came to join with our forces to stop the whole of Europe from being overtaken by "Jerry," the slang used to refer to Germans soldiers.

The Yanks used to sit on the steps of the town hall and around the village square. My sister, Gloria, was there one day speaking to some of the American soldiers. She was six years old with a head of gorgeous black, curly hair and the face of a doll. The Yanks told her that she was cute and asked if she had a big sister. She told them that she did and ran home excitedly to get me and take me to the square with her. She introduced me as her "big sister" and there was much laughter all around, as I was all of eight-years-old.

The town hall was used on Saturday nights to show movies to the local villagers and movie night was something to look forward to all week long. The war news played during intermission, which updated everyone about the things that were happening at the war front. Most news broadcasts were done in spurts of cheerful segments to raise the level of optimism. The propaganda raised morale and lifted spirits for the British and Yanks alike.

Those doses of positivity were much needed. The American airfields were such sad places when their pilots took off for bombing attacks over Germany. Those that were not scheduled to fly that day stood around and counted the planes that took off and they were back on the landing strips at night to count the planes that returned. They knew which of their buddies had taken off that morning and knew which planes did not come back. It was heartbreaking for them as they waited for the missing planes in hopes they might just be running late. Two of our favorite Yanks, Nelson and Sammy, did not return after one such flight. As young children, we were not told what happened to them, even though we missed them and asked about them throughout the war. Death surrounded us daily, but it was unnecessary to expose us to any more heartbreak.

Mum played piano well and when in Somerset with us, would go to the local pub and play. Many soldiers surrounded her as she played, singing their hearts out. However, many white American soldiers resented the fact that, in England, black American soldiers were welcome in pubs and dance halls. Fights often broke out due to the white soldiers' aggression and prejudice. The racial tension was palpable. Mum had not grown up exposed to segregation and explained to us that there was an official policy of segregation in the United States military. This racial discrimination and violence were often ugly and difficult for Mum to watch.

By this time, we had befriended many American soldiers. What a blessing they were to our family. They would come to our little cabin to bring cans of Spam, chocolate rations from their own kits, and comic books. Their wives and kids would send us the latest copies of magazines and we kept up with their American lifestyles. It was good for us to see there were some parts of the world where no bombs pounded homes and schools. Although it wasn't our normal, we were pleased that peace existed someplace. This is when I decided I wanted to go to America.

TOGETHER AGAIN

Mum could not bear parting with us any longer, so she came to Somerset with big brother Ivor and little Brian, to search for a place where we could all live together. She finally found a disused airfield base near Yeovil, South Somerset, about twenty miles away from her sister. Without a car or other forms of transportation at that time, this might as well have been a hundred miles away. On the base were two Quonset huts with their arced, corrugated tin roofs, which other evacuees had taken over. These huts had been soldiers' quarters during the First World War. Each tiny barracks room had bunk beds in them, and there was a long line of outdoor toilets just outside the dwelling.

The building Mum chose was constructed from wood and had a potbelly stove in it. We had no kitchen or cooking stove, so the potbelly stove became our all-purpose appliance. It was used to heat the hut, to cook meals with one pot at a time, and, of course, to make tea at teatime. We had our priorities.

One day, the fire in our stove dwindled, but we were hungry and needed a meal soon. Mum acted quickly and poured kerosene on the fire to rekindle it. The high flames blew up in her face. The explosion completely removed her eyebrows. It was a startling and scary sight. She felt lucky that her eyebrows were the only damage. For the remainder of her life, she drew on eyeliner to fill in her blank brows and she remained beautiful.

Kerosene lights were used as there was no electricity in the building, so Mum proceeded to wire the place herself. I will never forget the big moment when the lights were to be turned on for the first time. Kids were sent out into the field where there were cows and horses, and we were told to stand back in case of an explosion. Amazingly, the lights shined on, and everyone cheered in delight.

We didn't know it when we moved to the airfield base near Yeovil in 1945, but that would be the last year of the war.

VICTORY

I was 11 when the war came to an end in 1945. The celebrations were reminiscent of emotions that I had felt during the coronation of King George VI. There were wonderful victory parties throughout the streets of London and throughout all of Great Britain. A stage was built across from our home and many volunteers came from far and wide to get the grand party started. Coupon books were brought together to get the ingredients for cakes and tea. Tables were set up along each road, even outside the bombed-out homes. Union Jacks were displayed everywhere flapping patriotic red, white, and blue in the light breeze. Radios blared from every direction. The festivities were so joyous for all of us who had survived.

Mum and her friend, Gert, worked for days making dozens of paper roses in red, white, and blue to adorn the tables outside our house. Many helping hands put together taffeta dresses for Gloria and me for our upcoming sing-along on the stage. We had practiced our tune and we were nervous, but ready. When it was time for the two of us to get on the stage, we climbed the stairs, stood glued together, frozen. The pianist kept starting the song and we never joined her. We were terrified. I kept nudging Gloria, and she kept nudging me. The pianist gave up and played the song through to the end without any help from us, the two scared singers. Not a sound ever left our lips.

Our men and women from the forces were not home yet, but the festivities continued anyway. After more than five years of misery, it was shamefully easy in that moment of jubilation for our young minds to forget those who had not outlived the war.

For at least a year afterward, the children on the street played hide-and-seek in the rubble of the bombed houses. We were not supposed to, of course, as it was dangerous, but we did so anyway. Walls and stairs sometimes fell to the ground when we jumped or dove to hide behind the jagged walls. One day while we played, we found an unexploded bomb that lay on what was left of the living room floor of one of the houses. We realized then that it was indeed an extremely dangerous place to play. The air raid wardens, who were still on duty for that very reason, were called in to dismantle and take away the bomb. We were a lot more wary after that, but our games continued in our old playing fields where the ack-eack-ack anti-aircraft guns had still not been taken away.

Dad came home in early 1946 after his demobilization from the RAF. Life was expected to return to some normalcy as everyone tried to get used to being together again, but it did not all go smoothly. Dad had left for India in 1942 when Brian was a newborn, and he came back to a four-year old boy who did not know him other than as a strange man suddenly living in the house. Until Brian was an adult, there was little rapport between him and Dad. Gloria was also quite young when Dad left, and she too responded to him with difficulty after he first returned. Dad did nothing to make the transition easier for any of us.

BEING JEWISH

Our parents had not told us we were Jews until after the war. There was so much antisemitism, and everyone feared that the Nazis would win the war. For our own safety, my parents thought it was better that we did not know we were Jewish. Consequently, while evacuated in Somerset, we went to Sunday school each week and I enjoyed the stories about the loved and respected man named Jesus. After the war, Mum told us of our religion, although we were not practicing Jews.

When I returned to school there were only four girls out of four hundred students who were Jewish: me, Gloria, Freda, and one other young lady. Freda was a classmate who became a friend. Freda was a deeply religious girl and asked me if I would like to go to synagogue with her each week to learn Hebrew. I had nothing better to do, so I went along.

The synagogue was at the end of a residential street, so we had to walk past many rowhouses to get there. The women and their children would come out into their gardens and throw stones at the Jewish boys and girls as they passed by. It was appalling. I never forgot the horror that I witnessed of such ingrained hatred in those British women and how they modeled this behavior to their children. As a result, I did not continue Hebrew school.

Meanwhile, Christian religious lessons were the norm in our school. A German woman taught our class and repeatedly told the class that Jesus was killed by the Jews. To press her point, she glared at Freda and me, knowing our Jewish descent. After hearing this story told over and over, I went home and asked Mum if I could skip religious classes. She understood the problem fully and went to the headmaster to ask for me to be excused. The headmaster was very understanding and let me take a class of my choice for that hour each week. I took shorthand.

Although I never practiced Judaism, I grew to understand my heritage and its importance to me. Over the years, my family learned more of the Jewish customs and holiday celebrations, like Passover dinner, from my grandmother, who we affectionately called our Bubbah.

JACK AND RENÉE

Jack was Dad's close friend since boyhood. He was a soldier during the War and one of the concentration camp rescuers when the liberation started in Germany. In one of the groups Jack rescued from a camp, there was a Jewish mother and her two adult daughters. Renée, one of the daughters, stole Jack's heart. She was completely bald, frighteningly thin, but sweet and intelligent and Jack was quite fond of her.

Their story was heart-wrenching. Both mother and daughter saw their husbands and father shot by the Nazis. The Jewish family had been owners of a very large, well- known, shoemaking factory in Germany. The Nazis had taken their factory before they killed their husbands and put the women in a concentration camp. Against the odds, all three women survived the harsh conditions in the camp. Once they were free, they needed basic things such as a place to live and good medical care. Jack got them to England and set them up with the help that they desperately needed.

By the time Renée had grown a tiny amount of hair and gained a few pounds on her rail-thin body, she and Jack were married in our house. It was a joyous occasion. When we considered the chances that her own mother and sister could be in attendance following the brutality and loss they had endured during the war, it was quite amazing.

A few years later, with legal papers in hand, Renée and Jack went back to Germany to try to reclaim Renée's family business. It was somewhat of a battle in the courts for proof of ownership and there was plenty of paperwork and red tape. Their trust in the German legal system was not great, but the courts came through. Renée, her mother, her sister, and Jack came out of the court with the ownership documents in hand. They all went to dinner to celebrate the big win.

An hour after dinner, Jack suddenly dropped to the pavement, dead of a heart attack. Renée, her mother, and her sister were in disbelief. They had just toasted their success moments earlier. The shock was so terrible to bear for his family and friends. They brought his body back to England for his funeral, which was the first I had ever attended and the sadness we shared was without end. Devastated and widowed, Renée decided to return to Germany.

IVOR

My big brother, Ivor, was 14-years-old at the end of the war. He took his school exams that allowed him to enter a higher learning establishment and continue his studies until he turned 18. This could have opened better opportunities in later years for him. However, although he passed his tests with flying colors, he was Jewish. His spot in the better school was offered to a Christian boy even though his marks were not as high as Ivor's. The school did not seem at all ashamed to tell this to my parents.

When Ivor left school, he went to work in London at the head offices for a theater company, Granada Cinemas. He started as an office boy and advanced to a more pivotal role where he secured research material for the screenwriters to ensure the scenes were authentic for the period. He worked there for five years and got to know the actors. Ingrid Bergman, Joseph Cotton, Michael Wilding, and Alfred Hitchcock were only a few of the film stars that Ivor got to know.

During this time, Ivor joined the Air Training Cadets for three years and spent his holidays in RAF camps in England. One of his training sessions included a flight over Germany to see the devastation the RAF had inflicted during World War II. On one of Ivor's night flights, the brake hydraulics failed during the landing approach. The aircraft hurled towards the glass front flight control building on touchdown. Miraculously one brake suddenly engaged as they slid sideways and crashed into a plane on the tarmac. The propellers tore through the other plane's cockpit, which was empty, thankfully. When the aircraft doors opened, Ivor and four other young men staggered out shaken and in disbelief. They walked away with only bruises and quite a story to tell.

Later, Ivor was trained as a wireless operator and passed the proficiency exams. That training gave him the opportunity to become a radio transmitter operator when he was called up into the RAF in 1950. Ivor was sent to Egypt to help protect British interests in the Suez Canal Zone during a time of rising Egyptian nationalism. The Egyptians did not like that the British were there and continuously attacked their camp. After being stationed there for six months, Ivor was moved to Iraq during an oil crisis. He was in constant contact with the Royal Navy wireless operators in the Gulf. The camp was based 50 miles west of Baghdad, in the city of Habbaniyah and was like a holiday camp in comparison to Egypt. The Iraqi people were grateful to have the RAF there, unlike the Egyptians who resented the English presence.

Three months later, Ivor returned to Egypt to complete his last months of service. While waiting to set sail, Ivor heard that the local Egyptian police and students had started to attack the base again. Two British Army tanks moved into town and gave the police an ultimatum: "Stop the attacks and surrender your weapons or our tanks will wreck your headquarters." The Egyptian police refused, so British tanks drove straight through the building.

There was blood shed on both sides over the next few years culminating in the Suez Crisis, but, by then, Ivor had already left Egypt. I was grateful for his safe return. We survived one war together and I could not bear the thought of losing him in that crisis.

FREDA

While abroad, Ivor and my school girlfriend, Freda, wrote to each other constantly. Freda had suffered from mental disabilities as a child and had been in institutions several times during her teen years. I befriended her primarily because of our shared Jewish heritage. Before Ivor left to go abroad in the RAF, he asked Mum to forbid me to spend time with Freda because he thought she was quite crazy. He was correct. However, Freda got his address and started writing to him. By the time he came home a year later, Ivor was ready to date. During his deployment and, perhaps because of her letter campaign, he changed his mind about Freda. However, not much had changed about Freda, herself.

Whenever Ivor went to her house to pick her up for a date, she timed him. If he didn't arrive at the appointed time, she would call us on the phone and threaten that if he wasn't there in the next five minutes, she would kill herself. Mum heard this idle threat repeatedly, until Mum had enough of it and replied, "Why don't you wait a few minutes and I'll be right there to help you?" Freda did not pull that nonsense again, but interactions like these took its toll on our family.

It seemed Freda was jealous of the kind of love our family shared. Our bonds were solid and unwavering. Ivor played the piano beautifully from Beethoven to Boogie Woogie and after dinner we would gather around the piano and ask him to give us a tune. Each time this happened, Freda stayed on his lap and did not let him move. She seemed to always want control over him. Then she would feign a headache and would insist on going home. We never got to hear him play again once Freda and he were dating. She did not want to share him with anyone.

We were never invited to her home, nor were our parents asked to meet hers, even as Freda and Ivor's romance progressed. Ivor never joined in any of our family parties or gatherings again. She simply would not allow it. Freda had complete control over him. I was heartbroken as I felt I had lost my brother.

Despite the friction with our family, Freda became a big part in helping my brother Ivor grow his photography business over the years. Before color prints were available, watercolors were used to colorize the black and white prints by hand, and Freda became an expert at the process. Ivor photographed weddings and bar mitzvahs for many years. Freda was an integral part of the business.

Our family continued to reach out to her over the years, but Freda's behavior was neurotic, irrational, and controlling. Unfortunately, her mental instability and possessiveness caused a great rift in our family. It was difficult to tell if her actions were out of deliberate meanness or just a lack of empathy, but the effect was the same. Freda pushed people away, away from herself, and away from my brother. Regardless, he loved her dearly and looked beyond her faults.

A HELPING HAND

Once Dad was back home, our life had some stability to it. However, for others, circumstances were not so reliable. After the war, many people had fallen on hard times and both Mum and Dad were compassionate toward those who might need a little help.

Mum was ill and in hospital just after the war's end. While there, she took pity on Maud, a young woman who was recovering from a miscarriage. Maud's husband was physically abusive to her, and she did not dare go back to him. Furthermore, Maud's only living relative was her mother, who was in a mental asylum. She had no one to turn to.

I was 12-years-old when Mum brought Maud home to live with us. Mum asked her to help around the house and with the children occasionally. Shortly after Maud's arrival, ironically, she got a job at a condom factory. It was such fun for us when she would come home with condoms that had accidentally dropped into her shoes or purse. We thought they were balloons and would fill them with water and throw them at walls outside to watch them burst.

One evening when Mum was out and we were up in our rooms playing, I went downstairs for a drink of water and to use the bathroom. I discovered Dad and Maud in a compromising position on the couch. Although it did strike me as odd, I preferred not to acknowledge what I had seen and just rushed back upstairs. Nine months later, Maud gave birth to a gorgeous baby girl with all of Maud's likenesses. The baby was so precious with her blue eyes and blonde hair. She was named Patricia. Maud was in a terrible predicament and felt she had to put the baby up for adoption. Mum was so heartsick for the baby that she went to the official adoption agency and offered to adopt Patricia. Mum knew that the child was possibly Dad's, but those were the days before DNA tests and there was no way to prove it. Mum really did not care at that point and wanted to be a mother to the little girl. The adoption agency turned her down because they said that Maud would always know where to find her child should her personal circumstances improve. In those days, adoption was closed and final. When a woman gave up her baby, she never saw him or her again as long as she lived.

The dreadful day came when little Patricia was to be taken away. She was then six months, and we had all grown to love her dearly. It was a heart-wrenching day. Many tears were shed by all of us. Baby Patricia was adopted, Maud changed her name to Barbara Wren and went in search of a new life along with her new identity.

At about the same time that Maud arrived in our home, Nellie also became a close friend of my parents. Mum's best friend, Gert, had a handsome and wonderful son named Bert Jr. He had been a navigator for the RAF throughout the war and had met Nellie shortly thereafter. Nellie was still married to a soldier who was also quite abusive, and she longed to divorce and marry Bert Jr.

Adultery was the only way to get a divorce in the 1940's. At Nellie's request, Mum went to court and swore that Nellie had been an adulteress. Mum wrangled with this decision to get involved and how it might affect her friend, Gert, but it was the only way Nellie could get her freedom to marry Bert Jr. Of course, it was an easy decision for the judge to grant divorce rights to Nellie's husband with no alimony payments owed to her.

When Nellie and Bert Jr. finally married, it was a joy to the whole family. Unfortunately, Bert Jr. died of lung cancer shortly after their daughter Pam was born. Nellie was left alone with a big responsibility. Dad came forward and pleaded Nellie's case to the powers that be. Dad told of her husband, a veteran of World War II who had died very soon after the war. Dad explained that this left his widow and baby to an unknown life with no income. The War Department came through with some good benefits. Nellie was able to go back to work and become the provider, and Pam was able to go to a prestigious girl's school when she was old enough.

While Mum and Dad were at Waterloo Station awaiting a train, a young man started to chat with my mother. He wore his British Navy uniform, had a duffle bag over his shoulder, and said that he had come home from the war to a bombed-out house and no living relatives. Thanks to my parents' generosity, he became the next lodger in our house.

In that era, shillings were paid directly into a gas meter to provide gas for our stove and hot water heater. When the gas man came to collect the shillings, there were none in the gas meter under the stairs. For weeks, we hadn't noticed that the coins were being emptied by our new friend. We learned shortly thereafter that our lodger had been in prison for one thing or another for the entire length of World War II.

After the War, the government provided demobilization suits, including a shirt, tie, and shoes to each of the servicemen when heading back into civilian life. This man must have been wearing a "borrowed" British Navy uniform when our parents first met him at the train station. His authentic clothing tricked us into believing his sad homecoming tale.

One day, while our family was away from home, the con man was taken away. Back to prison he went. It wasn't until the day after he was gone that my father went to put on his own demobilization suit and found the whole ensemble missing.

SONG AND DANCE

There was often a subtle battle of sorts that took place in our house. Mum played piano and loved to keep up with the latest pop songs. Meanwhile, not to be outdone, Dad would blare classical music on the radio in the next room. Of course, all the kids loved the latest tunes more, and were constantly mad at Dad when he played the radio so loudly. We would all laugh about this non-verbal fighting between our parents.

Dad determinedly introduced me to classical music. On one occasion when the entire family was out except Dad and me, he told me, "Stop scrubbing the kitchen floor. Come and sit down. Listen to this piece of music that is on the radio." He was playing Beethoven's 5th piano concerto, better known as the "Emperor Concerto." I told him that I didn't want to hear it and would rather clean the floors. At his insistence, I finally sat down on the settée in front of the fire. There was no other light in the room but for the dancing flames that made shadows on the ceiling and walls. I sat angrily and wondered how I could escape from listening to such stodgy music.

Gradually, as the sound filled the room, it also filled my heart with a joy I had never known. I was richer for all that I experienced during that next hour. Tears tumbled down my cheeks as the melody continued. I never wanted it to end.

As the years went by, I became an ardent fan of Beethoven, then Mozart, Dvorak, Vivaldi, and many other composers who could lift my spirits. I remained eternally grateful to Dad for making me listen. To think of the joy I would have missed all my life if I had, as a stubborn child, outright refused him and gone back to cleaning the kitchen floor. There was room in my heart for both old and new music which has remained a big part of my life.

Of course, the big hits of the day were still high on my list of priorities. All work came to a halt when something popular was on the radio. We all danced around the living room with a broom, mop, or whatever was at hand. Those were such gay and happy times in our home.

Mum was a great dancer. Ballroom dancing was another passion of hers and she taught us all the latest steps. When we became teenagers, our parents took us to the dance halls where everyone dressed in long gowns and danced the minuet, Scottish reel, and old-fashioned waltz. I danced a jig on one occasion, and my slip started to slowly fall to the ground. I was an easily embarrassed teenager, but somehow the laughter from my whole family and others who had seen the mishap disarmed me.

It was a grand, lovely, English pastime in which we didn't have to be of the aristocracy to engage. A live orchestra played and there was lots of laughter and excitement in the air. Dad always said he would not go to these dances but, thank goodness, he did because he had loads of fun, and it was good for us to see him in such high spirits.

Mum became more independent and started to go out on the town around London with her girlfriends. She was a magnificent dancer and loved to visit the grand ballrooms. She spent whole afternoons at swanky hotels while she sipped tea or cocoa and conversed with various people with whom she had become friendly. On at least two occasions, a man came into her life with whom she fell madly in love. By this time, Mum knew she no longer loved my father.

We knew she was unhappy at home. We begged her to start a better life for herself away from our father. Still, she would never get divorced or leave her children. Mum was always home by late afternoon to fix supper and never stayed out overnight. Regardless, I often had to lie to cover for Mum when she was somewhere that she did not want Dad to know about. As a direct result of the lies I was forced to tell to save Mum, I found it difficult to misrepresent my feelings or bend the truth thereafter.

Dad was totally despondent and heartbroken because Mum was out so much and had obviously lost all feeling for him. It saddened me greatly to sense his stress and to see him cry. However, he was verbally abusive toward Mum and treated her disrespectfully, so my feelings were conflicted. I loved my parents and wanted the best for each of them, but to live under these circumstances was not a happy situation. It was hard to believe when Mum told me they had been so happy during their first seven years together.

Somehow, despite all the arguments and unspoken tension between my parents, they maintained an amazing sense of humor. They were often telling funny jokes or playing cards into the late hours of the night with my Auntie Anne and Uncle Lou. Our family went on holidays to Southend-On-Sea and Somerset. Those spells of laughter interspersed with family gatherings kept us sane and hopeful that things would get better between our parents. Things did not improve, but there were many bright spots that made it all bearable.

TAILOR MADE

Regardless of all that happened between Dad and Mum and the many reasons for the slow disintegration of their marriage, to me my father was always the most loving of fathers. He made Gloria and me some of the loveliest clothes. We were the best dressed in our school, not due to wealth, but because we had such a talented father. He was a tailor for the designer department store, Liberty of London. As such, he was able to bring home all the scraps of luxurious material not used on whatever exclusive item he was making for some grand lady. His works were one of a kind and people paid dearly for them. He even created gowns for royalty and sometimes joined them for high tea.

Unfortunately, his wage was a pittance and Liberty of London and their famous designers were becoming rich from his hard labors. I once went to see a designers' show with gorgeous models prancing up and down the runway wearing garments Dad had made. As he was a tailor and not a designer, there was no applause for him at the end of the fashion show and I thought that a pity.

Mum had a good sense for business and offered to be Dad's partner in selling his beautiful handmade clothes. She would have been a great help to him. After she finished school, my mother worked for a millinery shop. She learned quite a lot, but marriage came along before she could use her new-found talent. Together, I believe they could have started their own business making incredible fashions. However, Dad declined Mum's offer and continued to work for Liberty of London.

COMING OF AGE

It was 1948 and I had become a teenager. The Second World War was in the past. At times, I felt full and magical and at others, sad and burdened. However, it was during those years that I began to discover my love of travel, which consisted of simple weeklong trips around England. At 14-years-old, I found myself in Somerset for a week's vacation with Gloria and our cousin, Marion. Naturally, I was shy about my changing body and what it lacked. My father made me a stunning pale blue fitted winter coat and sewed padding inside the lining on each bosom. It looked natural as long as the coat remained buttoned. The three of us met some boys at the playground in the park. Marion, who had no such need for extra padding, thought this was an ideal time to have some fun. I was bundled up in my new coat and completely content. Marion said, "Why don't you unbutton your coat, Elaine, soon you'll be feeling very hot." After nagging me incessantly, I unbuttoned my jacket. My padded bosoms flew out to each side of me. We were all bright red in the face and could not contain our laughter.

Another summer, Gloria, Rhoda, Cynthia, and I rented a tiny, hard-top caravan camper that was set up in a trailer park on the beach in Southend-on-Sea. We had great fun playing ball with two young fellows, until one of them jumped to catch the ball and fell backwards into a trash barrel. Rhoda wet herself straight through her skirt from the laughter. Two of us got behind her and one in front to shield her embarrassment. As we got inside the caravan, she slipped into the bunk area and pulled the privacy curtain so she could change into dry clothes. We tried to occupy the blokes with conversation. We asked Rhoda if she was okay. She replied that nothing was the matter as she threw her garment over the privacy curtain rail. Her skirt was dangling with the tell-tale wet stain for all to see. The rest of us laughed so hard that we all nearly wet ourselves.

On a particular trip by the seaside, these same friends and I experienced an unexpected turn of events. We went to stay in a caravan close to the ocean on the Cliffs of Dover, high above the water's edge. We ventured down to the beach and slowly made our way to a quiet area below the cliffs. It was lovely to feel the gentle breeze and listen to the waves as we lay stretched out on our beach towels.

When three of us wandered away from the beach, my sister Gloria remained behind to enjoy the calm and the salty smell of the ocean. My friends and I went to the top of the cliff where we called and waved down to Gloria. By this time, the tide was coming in strong and fast. This sudden change caught us all by surprise. We could see that Gloria was pressed up against the cliff wall with the water approaching quickly. Rhoda and Cynthia hurried to hunt down some food while I went to the little fishing village to find a fisherman who was willing to go on a dangerous trip around jagged rocks and heavy seas to rescue Gloria. I was beyond grateful when one obliged.

I joined the girls on the cliffside. We attempted to throw a package of food down to Gloria, but the wind was far too strong and blew it directly back to us. We tied stones to the package and managed to get it down to her. The kind fisherman successfully rescued Gloria.

We were so thankful for Gloria's safety once we were reunited that we just hugged and cried together. She ended up with strep throat for over a week. It could have been much worse, and I refused to let my mind wander to what could have happened to my little sister.

This was the first of a handful of difficult but valuable lessons I learned throughout my life about the life-threatening power of the sea. I always loved being by the sea and these trips further cultivated my love for travel throughout my life.

WORKING WORLD

At 15, I finished school, which was the norm in Britain in the late 1940s. Months later, in February of 1950, I started my first full-time job in London. I worked in the mailroom of a magazine publishing company that was down the street from Big Ben. I would often escape the office and enjoy my lunch near the magnificent clock. A staff member held a weekly class where we were taught how to proficiently use a typewriter. I also attended technical college at night to master shorthand, typing, and English to help me get secretarial work.

On my first day of work, my brother's friends, Stan and Maurice, took me on the train and buses to make sure I arrived safely. They were kind and protective, which made me feel much more confident than if I had been alone and worried about getting lost.

Many of the girls in the mailroom often hassled me about my Jewish heritage. I never found out how they knew I was Jewish. They felt it was the fault of the Jews that their fathers or brothers had served in the British forces. Their wrongful opinions were promoted by propaganda put out by British officials who also blamed Jews. I tried to make it clear to my coworkers that my father had also fought in the war, but my efforts to end their accusations were to no avail.

The kind lady who managed the mailroom gave me the lovely opportunity to take my lunch hour during a parade of the royal family across the River Thames. I took a bus there and found the streets packed with thousands of people waiting to cheer for King George, Queen Elizabeth, young Princess Elizabeth, and Princess Margaret along the route. These moments of viewing an imperial procession always felt like a treasure to me.

As I neared the crowd, I could only see large groups of people, twenty deep and I could not yet view the road where the carriage was to pass. Various kind people urged me to the front of the line, until I landed in a perfect spot, not far from the curb. The royal guards lined the road on both sides and stood at attention with their rifles and bayonets at their sides. Their tall, bushy, black hats made them appear like giants to me. Within minutes, down the line, an order was given by their chief guard and rifles were slung over their shoulders with precision and pageantry. I stood directly behind one of them. Then I realized why people let me go to the front. In a flash, the bayonet swooped directly over my head, skimming my hair within an inch. I had not yet grown to five-foot tall, so I did not get beheaded.

To see the beautiful golden coach go by slowly with the stunning royal family in all their glory was a sight I could never forget. They waved at the crowd and lifted our spirits. Seeing the monarchy up close gave me a strong sense of patriotism. I felt so privileged when I got back to the mailroom. Of course, I could not talk about it to the other girls as I did not want to cause trouble for the head of the mailroom who had given me permission to go. When I returned home, I raved about it to my family.

I rode regularly to and from work on London's trains, which was a boost to my independence and was sometimes a bit of an adventure. There was an unusual luxury at Liverpool Street Station. Bathroom facilities were provided for a small fee and I could get a towel, washcloth, and a tiny compartment with a bath of hot water. It was rather convenient to use this clever comfort station if I planned to go out after work. That way, I didn't have to spend hours of travel time to go home to clean up for a night on the town. Since I lived forty-five minutes away from where I worked, I often carried a change of clothes with me and used this handy washroom on various occasions.

Frequently I knit while commuting on the train. My knitting bag tucked easily under my arm and it was a relaxing and productive pastime. One evening I headed home from work and barely caught the departing train at Liverpool Station. Each train car was fully loaded so I scurried down the long train platform to find a vacant seat. I noticed people sitting in the train waving and laughing at me. At the last carriage I was able to hop on the train step as a fellow passenger kindly helped open the door for me to enter.

Slowly, I discovered the reason for the laughter. At the very beginning of the race, unbeknownst to me, as I was running, I had dropped a full ball of yarn on the platform. By the time I entered the train, I only had knitting needles in my bag. The ball of yarn had bounced and chased me from behind leaving an awfully long length of blue yarn strung clear through the Liverpool Street Station.

❖   ❖   ❖

During 1950, I decided to join the Women's Volunteer Services (WVS), which had existed since 1938. I was 16 and eager to lend a helping hand. There was a huge demand for help when the war ended, and thousands of people needed clothes and food for their families. The Marchioness of Reading, known as Lady Reading, was founder and chair of this group. She was also a former British Ambassador to the United States and was involved with many other philanthropic organizations. By the end of the War, WVS was over a million women strong and was hailed as the "Greatest Women's Army in the World." There was so much to do to repair our country.

After work, I spent hours at the distribution center where I sorted clothes into categories by size and gender, separated children's wear from toys, or organized food. The work seemed endless. Food had to be stored properly for short periods of time to give to the needy customers, who came in daily. There were those who tried to take advantage of the kindness and we discovered that some had taken the clothes and sold them. Desperation has a way of making people do things that seem out of character.

I worked alongside many elderly women and enjoyed the camaraderie. I was told that I was the youngest volunteer in the country for this cause. After hundreds of hours, I earned the badge of WVS and was immensely proud of it. Lady Reading gave me the badge personally with a little speech thanking me. I was quite touched and extremely honored.

When I was sure I knew my way around London on the buses and underground system, I ventured to a nursing home for war veterans. They treated me as they would a grandchild. I loved hearing their war stories and about their lives in other countries. I found their tales fascinating. One of the older men had been instrumental in finding a treatment for malaria. I did not realize it at the time, but that man was likely Hans Andersag who discovered chloroquine, the active ingredient in the malaria drug Resochin. Others told of battles which involved hand-to-hand combat with German soldiers. They told sorrowful tales of their friends dying right beside them. Their stories filled me with awe and the desire to do more for them, for those we allow to slip away without glory.

40

DANCE HALLS

A year or so later, Gloria, our friend Rhoda, and I would go to the big band dance halls where we danced our feet off and met all kinds of young blokes from different cultures around the world. We danced with many handsome American soldiers. It was pure and innocent fun. At one dance, we met some lovely Greek and Cypriot fellows. As usual, we extended an invite to everyone with whom we went out to come to our home for dinner or tea. My parents were wonderful at entertaining all of the young foreign men who came over. Our house was very cosmopolitan, and each group taught us something about their various customs, dances, and religions.

One evening at the dance hall, we met some young Pakistani men. India and Pakistan had recently become two independent countries. These young men were close-knit with their community in London. The Prime Minister of Pakistan was soon to visit their embassy and the fellows invited us to this honorable occasion. We accepted.

The evening at the Pakistan Embassy was quite special. The women in their colorful saris were a delight to behold. We patiently waited in the reception room with a huge crowd of welcoming guests. We waited for over an hour for Prime Minister Liaquat Ali Khan to appear. Gloria's feet ached from her high-heeled shoes, so she slipped them off. With such a crowd around us, no one noticed. Then, suddenly the double doors swung open into the reception room and the Prime Minister of Pakistan gallantly appeared. The first people in the reception line shook hands with him while Gloria bent over to put on her shoes, but she struggled to find them on the floor amidst the crowd. I began giggling like crazy when I realized that my sister's bum in the air was what greeted the Prime Minister. I cannot remember if she ever did shake his hand.

Tragically, Prime Minister Liaquat Ali Khan was assassinated in 1951, merely four years after his election.

NAZARUDDIN

During these teenage years, my friend Rhoda and I met two wonderful fellows named Mazlim and Osman. They were from the British protectorate of Malaya. Rhoda quickly fell in love with Mazlim, who was from the Capital of Malaya, Kuala Lumpur. Her parents forbade her to continue a romantic relationship with him because of her Jewish heritage. She secretly kept on with the relationship. We brought both of the fellows home to meet my Mum and Dad and we all got along famously. They asked if they could bring one of their fellow countrymen the next time they visited, and we were happy to welcome him. They were enrolled at the prestigious Sandhurst Military Academy in London, the equivalent of West Point in the United States. When they graduated, they would become officers destined to return to British Malaya, as Malaysia was known then, to fight against the Chinese Communists.

Nazaruddin was the young man they brought on their next visit to my home. He was handsome, elegant, and a true gentleman. I fell for him immediately and he for me. Mazlim and Osman told us that in their country, they would not be allowed to enter or leave a room in his presence without bowing to him. We were surprised to learn that his given name was Prince Ungku Nazaruddin. We called him Ruddin. He did not reveal his background, so we treated him as we did everyone else.

When Ruddin and I fell in love, there followed an incredible romance the likes of which fairy tales are written. He and I would meet during my lunch hour from work. He would send a London taxi for me and we'd enjoy a wonderful Indian, French, or Chinese meal. We would flirt and swoon over one another during these breathtaking meetings. Then, I would be whisked back to work by another black cab. I often felt out of breath and happy beyond words. After work, he would meet me in London and take me to many delightful restaurants, movies, plays, and picnics in Hyde Park. Our courtship was magical. We were truly in love, and I always found parting to put a deep ache in my heart.

Ruddin escorted me to very elegant and prestigious dances at the Malay embassy. It was the custom for any other man who wished to dance with me to ask Ruddin, not me, for permission. He would add the man's name to the dance card upon his approval. I did not drink liquor at all, but Ruddin would order champagne for me. I'd place the full flutes under my chair, so as not to be rude or embarrass him. It was only when I was out on the dance floor that I noticed the very visible, full line of glasses under my chair. As I had tried not to embarrass him, I had embarrassed myself instead.

Ruddin was an extremely jealous man, and it was difficult for me to handle this temperamental side of his personality. On one occasion, I stood on an escalator going down to meet him during rush hour. I had to stand still as it was very crowded. It happened that there was a man both in front of and behind me on the escalator. When I reached the bottom, Ruddin was extremely angry and said I had been with two men. He said he saw me flirting with them. He could be terribly brash. On another occassion we went to a French restaurant that I remarked was "very nice," to which he answered that he would take "any cheap tart" there. I was so highly offended that I left and took the first train home. He called my father to explain and apologize.

Our romance took many turns before he took me to the Strand, a part of London's diamond district. He bought me a stunning engagement ring and I was happily overwhelmed. I said yes to his proposal, despite the red flags. My rose-colored glasses were certainly disguising some inherent traits that were disagreeable to me. I was, but 17-years- old at the time and would have had to wait another year before I could even consider leaving for Malaya to marry him.

Ruddin invited me to attend his graduation ceremony from Sandhurst Academy. King George VI of England would hand out the diplomas to the graduates. The Queen Consort and several royal family members would be attending to congratulate them. The attendance of the royal family was a great honor. I could barely wait to curtsey the dainty way Mum had instructed me.

I was both thrilled and stunned to be attending such a grand affair. The gala event was to be held on the impressive grounds at Sandhurst. To receive an invitation, one must be royalty and my fiancé was Prince of Kuala Lumpur. I had to pinch myself. Dad made me my very first evening gown for the occasion. It looked rich and very elegant, and I felt like a Princess when I tried it on. I dreamt of the graduation day and was excited to attend the gala with royalty. On the big day I would leave my publishing job and head to the Liverpool Street train station to take a paid bath. I could change into my gown at the station, then head to Sandhurst with Ruddin. I was exuberant and could barely wait.

The day of the gala finally arrived. When I got to work there was lots of chatter. I was stunned when I heard the news from everyone that King George VI had died suddenly of a coronary thrombosis in his sleep. King George VI had so valiantly seen us through the long, horrific years of World War II. I was devastated. Selfishly, I was more upset about losing my chance to go to Sandhurst for the most exciting event of my life. I had been looking forward to this day for so long and in a flash discovered that I would not be able to attend the big gala.

I immediately felt dreadful about my selfish attitude. In spite of my religious background, I went to the huge church across from my workplace. I sat alone on a very long pew and prayed for the King's soul. I was deeply ashamed of myself for my uncharacteristic and self-centered reaction. How was I more upset that I was denied this beautiful event than that our beloved king had perished? I found great solace at the church and was grateful to be alive.

Months later, Nazaruddin said goodbye to our family before his return to Malaya. This left a gaping hole in my heart as Malaya was six thousand miles away and we had no plans for our next rendezvous. He was returning to a warzone, and I feared for his survival. I had endured war and knew too well of the potential tragedies and losses.

Mazlim and Osman departed a few weeks after Ruddin. Before their departure, Mazlim said something strange to me, "Too bad Prince Nazaruddin is still not free, in the Judeo-Christian sense, to marry you." I was confused and immediately questioned this. Mazlim confessed that Ruddin was already a married man. My heart sank to a depth I had not known. I was in shock and disbelief. I was stunned and disappointed that Ruddin had kept this vital information from me. After doing a bit of research, I learned that in the Muslim religion in Malaya, it was customary to have four wives as long as each wife was separately housed. I would be his second wife and over time, one of possibly four wives. That was totally against my beliefs and unimaginable.

Months after they had returned to Malaya, I discovered more about Nazaruddin. My brother Ivor had a South African friend, Jim, from the RAF. He had access to the files kept at Somerset House where foreign nationals were registered. Jim took a risk by looking into Nazaruddin's file and shared with me more about his background.

Nazaruddin had been seventeen-years-old during World War II, when the Japanese had invaded Malaya in December of 1941 and occupied it for the remainder of the war. He was fluent in Japanese and was an interpreter between the Malays and the British. He did not let the Japanese know that he spoke their language. He was a food server in their camp. Without showing interest in their daily actions and discussions, Nazaruddin acquired a great deal of knowledge of their plans. He went into the bush a few times a week to find the British freedom fighters who hid there. He shared valuable information with the army, and consequently and perhaps because of the intelligence Ruddin provided, the British retook that part of Malaya. As he had performed this highly dangerous mission at such a young age, Nazaruddin was awarded the Victoria Cross and other medals at Buckingham Palace.

Further research revealed that he was indeed married, and I finally approached him about this by mail. Still another story unfolded. His father had died young in life, so Nazaruddin went to live with his father's brother and family. He grew up with his cousins as though they were his own sisters and brothers. When the Japanese occupied Malaya, they had what they called "rest houses" set up in their camps. They were occupied with young Malay women. After being forced into having hysterectomies, they would become the sexual partners of the male Japanese soldiers. Ruddin's female cousin was sixteen and in training to become a nurse. Only single women were taken into the camps and his cousin was still single. His uncle begged Nazaruddin to marry his daughter to save her from the camps. Nazaruddin abided by his uncle's wishes only to save his young cousin from the potential brutality that she would face at the Japanese rest houses.

Ruddin promised me that if he was alive at the war's end, he would have the marriage annulled. At the time I learned the full story, the war had been over for quite some time and there was no annulment in sight. He claimed that she was merely like a sister in his eyes. However, I felt he would have said anything at that point to save our relationship. It was clear there was no chance we could overcome our cultural differences and I did my best to move on.

Years later, my mother admitted that I had received many letters from Nazaruddin. However, she had burned them to spare me more of a broken heart. She felt that no good would come of me reading his letters.

Seventy years later, after dear Rhoda had died, her daughter Dena found the most beautiful love letter to Rhoda from Mazlim. It was fifteen pages long. It was written over a long period of time from a journal he had kept after their farewells. Upon reading his words I was brought back to the warm gatherings we had shared in my home. He spoke about my family and how welcome the three of them felt in our presence. They had not been shown that deep warmth anywhere during their travels in England. It felt joyful for me to relive that special time in my young post war life.

In the letter, Mazlim also mentioned that he had questioned how Nazaruddin's mother would have treated me over the years had we been married. Would I have been welcomed and shown love? During our relationship she had sent me a beautiful sari, and I wrote to thank her. That was the extent of our correspondence.

After reading Mazlim's poetic and revealing love letter to Rhoda, I wondered if my mother had given me the love letters that Ruddin had written to me, perhaps I would have learned more about his way of life. I contemplated if I could have ever felt at home with him in Malaya had he gotten the promised annulment. I had been so in love with him, and these were the unanswerable questions that forever ran through my thoughts. I have accepted that there are some things I will never know.

HOSTESS

After Ruddin left, our lovely friend, Nellie, stepped in to help me mend my grieving heart. Nellie had loved and lost Bert Jr., so she knew my sorrow. I was quite a mess and didn't want to do anything, go anywhere, or stop crying. Nellie decided it was time for me to start living again. She had heard of a hostess program for the American airmen who were homesick and feeling the pressure of being so far from their families.

As hostesses, our part was to boost their morale. There were plenty of guidelines to keep it clean. To join, we had to have a "passport" with us, which needed to be signed by parents or guardians, a minister, and a supervisor from our workplace. The strict rules did not allow any serviceman to leave the dance hall with a girl at any time. All dancing and conversation were to be done within sight of the chaperones. To get to the military base we met outside the American embassy in London on Friday evening each week. A bus drove us on the hour-long trip to the base and we had to be on that bus to return after the dance. No hanging around or smooching with the young airmen was allowed, strictly dancing and chatting.

On our first trial of this new venture, my sister Gloria and I made our way to the American embassy and saw the bus up ahead, waiting for us stragglers who were running late. While racing to the bus, my panties fell around my ankles right in front of the guards at the doors of the embassy. I was totally mortified, but Gloria did not miss a stride. She kept running, shouting, "I don't know you! But don't worry, I'll hold the bus" I quickly stepped out of the panties, picked them up, and ran to the bus. A young airman stood in the doorway and requested to see our passports, but I was so flustered that I handed him my panties. I finally got the passport out of my purse and showed him. I was ushered to the back of the bus where all the girls offered to help me get myself back together using safety pins or anything that would hold the broken elastic on my panties together. I begged the girls not to tell anyone at the dance about this mishap. They teased me relentlessly and I'm sure the whole base knew about my misadventure. We all had a good laugh.

When we arrived at the dance, there, in the crowd of young airmen, a handsome man approached me and asked what I would like to drink. Only tea, coffee or soda was allowed. He kindly brought me a soda. We talked and danced the night away. After I left, he had somehow gotten my phone number from someone. I believe it was from my sister. I felt a sense of hope and a glimpse of life after Ruddin.

LONDON FOG

In December of 1952, the worst fog in London's history overtook our streets just as people were leaving work to head for home. The bus I rode was full of people coughing trying to gulp in fresh air, but there was none to be had. The bus driver needed the ticket conductor to take the kerosene lantern out and walk in front of the bus to light the way. On a clear day, we could have walked faster than the driver could advance through the dense cloud.

Riders were then asked to leave the bus, as it was too dangerous to drive, and everyone got off. Nothing could be seen at all, not even my hand held up to my face to cover my mouth. Some people around me headed to Liverpool Street Station, so I blindly followed their voices and gratefully found my way there. The steam trains still ran, and I was able to go to Walthamstow by railway. Once there, I pressed on, strictly by feel. I hung onto front-yard fences of houses and hoped memory would get me to my street. From the beginning of Elmfield Road, I felt for gate numbers at each house and traced the number with my fingers. I was relieved to finally find number sixteen, my own home at last.

That fog, or smog, as they started to call it, lasted five days and nights wreaking havoc and smothering London. Cows were dying in fields; sporting events and film showings were canceled. Road, air, and rail travel came to a halt. Hospitals were inundated with sick people who were unable to breathe when they were overcome by the polluted air. According to reports, as many as 12,000 people died from the toxins.

Prime Minister Churchill deemed it "God's Will," but scientists had a different version of what we were experiencing. Industrial chimney stacks as well as home fires that were fueled by coal were the real blame for the lethal smoke and fog mixture. An anticyclone had settled over London which trapped colder air under the warm air. It was the emissions of both domestic heating fires and factories trapped near ground level that produced the deadly toxins.

In 1956 the first Clean Air Act was passed as a direct response to the lethal fog. We could no longer use coal to light our fires. Electricity was used at a huge expense. Hot water pipes were placed in some rooms, mostly bathrooms, which also served well for drying towels and small pieces of washing. Electric heaters and hot water pipes could be turned on individually. Because electricity was relatively more expensive, we used those electric heaters sparingly in the rooms we occupied and turned them off upon vacating the room.

Churchill was nearly sacked for his inaction on the matter of the smog. However, when he visited the hospitals and saw the severity of the situation and how terribly it had impacted thousands of people, he resolved to be more engaged and thereby saved his own seat.

Riding in pram on May 12, 1937 London with sister Gloria and brother Ivor, enroute to the coronation of King George VI. Gloria on left, Elaine in center, Ivor on right.

My siblings and I running in Westcliff, England in the clothes my father made, 1938.

Mum, Rosalee Cheyney presented this gift to my father for keeping in his wallet during WWII while in India, 1939.

My father, Al Cheyney in his Royal Air Force Uniform heading to India, 1939.

Brother Ivor, sister Gloria and Elaine at 16
Elmfield Road, Walthamstow directly before
being whisked to the bomb shelter, 1942.

Gloria marching in the victory parade
on Elmfield Road, Walthamstow, 1945.

Sister Gloria, brother Brian and Elaine at war's end, 1945.

Elaine, Brian and Gloria at our 16 Elmfield Road doorstep wearing coats made by my father, 1946.

Fifteen-year-old Elaine in front of bombed out coal shed, 1949.

Holiday in Somerset, front left, Rhoda, front right, sister Gloria, back left, Elaine, back right, cousin Marion, 1950.

Elaine modeling a new
fashion dress made by Al in
1950.

Malayan Embassy porch with brother
Brian lower middle, Mazlam top left,
Prince Nazaruddin top middle, Osman
right, London, circa 1950.

Gloria, Stan, Elaine, Jason, Marion at the row houses, Walthamstow 1951.

Bubbah (dad's mother), Dad, Brian planning Elaine and Ron's wedding, 1953.

Freda, Gloria, Mum, Elaine at an
engagement party, 1953.

MOASCAR GARRISON
COURT MARTIAL
ROOM

Stan, Aubrey, Ivor, Maurice, joking at base on
Suez Canal in Egypt, 1954.

PART II

MARRIAGE

The handsome, young, American airman who had kindly brought me a soda when I was a hostess at the military base called me. His name was Ron Tarwater and our young romance blossomed quickly. I had not yet recovered from my broken heart with Nazaruddin. I wasn't ready to become serious with anyone at that time. However, Ron and I dated a few times and my family loved him. I was beginning to have feelings for him too. They kept asking him to speak to them because they loved his Midwestern American accent. I did too. He was a sweet and shy young man who was very homesick. All our hearts melted when he was around. Stan and Maurice took him under their wing. I was falling in love with this handsome American Air Force soldier.

When Ron proposed, I was completely stunned. He was only ten-months-older than me, we were both still so young at only 18. I told him we were too young, although I had been engaged before. I denied his proposal, however we continued to date. I enjoyed Ron's company, but I wanted to be sure of him. My first love with Ruddin made me cautious. After getting to know Ron better and earning my trust, he got down on one knee again. This time, I happily accepted his ring, I knew I was madly in love with him. However, our engagement was not entirely smooth.

We were at a public swimming pool not far from home. There was a black family swimming. Ron was mortified and could not imagine that black people were allowed in the same pool as whites. Horrified at his statements, I gave him back his ring and told him that I could not marry someone who felt that way. I discovered what blind prejudice really meant. Ron was brought up with that philosophy in western Missouri. He never thought to question the reasons behind these unjust divisions. We discussed the subject of prejudices at great lengths. Gradually his sweet kindness and understanding shone through. He was open minded and intelligent. I said yes to his proposal once again and we continued to plan our wedding day.

My parents were wonderfully supportive and worked very hard to give us a perfect day. Dad designed and made my stunning wedding gown. He and Gloria created all the bridesmaids' dresses. Mum sewed for hours to put sequins on various parts of my gown, crowned headdress, and veil. My sister Gloria and my friend Rhoda were my bridesmaids. A friend's daughter, Rita, was the flower girl. Ron asked his Air Force major to stand up for him, as his parents were in the States. Rudy, the other so-called confirmed bachelor, was his best man. My cousin Harold had a band and played for our wedding. We laughed and danced the night away. The festivities went strong until midnight.

At the end of the night, friends drove us into London to the Strand Hotel. We sat in the back seat and the car hit a tall curb at 35-miles-per-hour. We banged our heads very hard on the roof. Ron hurt his neck and I had a large bloody bump on my forehead. As we exited the car I said to Ron, "Try to act as though we didn't just get married." We entered the lobby of the Strand swarmed with people at nearly one in the morning. I was wearing my white gown, tiara, and veil, and Ron was in his tuxedo, so it was unlikely that we'd pull that fib off. We looked as though we had the most terrible wedding night brawl. We were terribly embarrassed.

Our luck did not improve the next morning. The two of us drove to Heathrow Airport to fly to Jersey Island in the English Channel for our honeymoon. There was a very dense fog and all planes were grounded for hours. I had never flown before and was excited and awed with this adventure. After hours of waiting, we boarded the plane. I was so thrilled to finally be flying.

During that era in England, we could buy tiny tins which contained small soapy pads called Quickies. They were used to freshen up. I wanted to feel fresh for the arrival at my honeymoon suite. As we were about to land, I removed a pad from the little tin and wiped my face and hands. I asked my groom if he would like a Quickie. His deadpan reply was, "Right now? Can't you wait until a bit later?"

On the Isle of Jersey, most people spoke English or French, but the waiters where we stayed were Greek and did not speak English well. After our lovely honeymoon night, we decided to have the ultimate luxury, breakfast served in bed. We ordered room service. While Ron shaved in the bathroom, I yelled for room service to enter. The waiter entered with an impressive silver tray held high in the air, which carried our breakfast, elegant silver food covers, linens, and fine silverware. There was an awkward, nonverbal moment as he searched around for where to set the tray down. At the same moment he leaned forward to set the tray on my bedside table, I jumped out of bed to help him. I whacked my head on the underside of the tray and everything flew all over me, the bed, and the floor. By the time Ron heard the commotion, I lay flat on the bed consumed by hysterical laughter. I tried to apologize to a person who could not understand a word I said, which made me laugh even harder. Ron and I were both laughing uncontrollably and ended up eating breakfast in the hotel restaurant. It was all very romantic.

We had planned to rent bikes and tour the Isle of Jersey as no motorized vehicles were allowed. I was a very inexperienced bike rider but thought it would be fun to give it a go. As luck would have it, I ran directly into a parked truck at the beginning of our adventure. I only received scratches and bruised my knees, so no big deal, as the Yanks would say. All in all, it was a memorable honeymoon, despites the bumps and bruises.

When we returned to normal life, we moved to Chiswick, London into an apartment at the top of a wonderful old three-story house. Two days before we moved in, an American Navy Captain and his wife moved from France into the flat below us. The couple who owned the house occupied the lower level.

While hanging the laundry on the line to dry in the garden, I met the young American Navy Captain. I welcomed him and suggested, "Knock me up any time if he needed anything." He went back to his flat and told his wife what their new neighbor had offered. I could not understand why they were both so cold to me. Neither of them spoke to me for over two months. Finally, when they did, they apologized and explained that they had learned from other British people that I was just being friendly and wasn't offering anything salacious. We shared lots of laughs over phrases like "keep your pecker up" and "take the piss." Thus, began the battle of British English versus American English, which would continue to be a battle that I would wage all my life.

Chiswick was a lovely area to begin our journey as a married couple. The house was perched upon the banks of the River Thames with a long, sweeping lawn leading to the river's edge. Close by were the beautiful Royal Botanic Gardens at Kew. There was much to do in our neighborhood that we did not need to be wealthy to enjoy. There was the beauty of nature surrounding us. The Oxford and Cambridge boat races were held on the River Thames each year. The finish line was at our new home which was so exciting for us. It was a special sight to see Princess Margaret on the opposite riverbank as she watched and cheered the racers to the finish.

We planned to remain in Chiswick for a year and then leave for America. Ron's family lived in Kansas City, Missouri which would be our first American destination. After the war, I always dreamt of living in America. I had grown fond of many of the American soldiers that had entered my life as a young girl. However, homesickness already loomed and I had yet to even leave England. Ron was understanding and kind. He had experienced the same feeling upon moving to England. When the time came to move, I was so upset about saying goodbye to my family that it took some of the joy out of the new adventure I had wanted most of my life. Consequently, before we even left the dock, I was hanging over the side of The General Maurice Rose, already getting sick.

It turned out to be the trip from hell. For the entire seven days of the crossing, I had non- stop seasickness. I could eat nothing but saltine crackers and even those I could not keep down. Men and women had separate sleeping quarters. As The General Maurice Rose was a troop ship, the cabin was barely big enough for one person, yet they had four women cramped in bunk beds.

There was no porthole, so I felt claustrophobic. Ron was great and never complained, even though he had to sleep in the hold of the ship in a swinging hammock with hundreds of other men that vomited all around him. He never got ill. Each day, he would come and get me so that I could walk with him on deck to get fresh air in the hopes it would make me feel better. Nothing made me feel better.

We finally arrived at Staten Island, New York, in the early hours of the morning. We never saw the greeting from the Statue of Liberty as it was shrouded in fog. We left the ship, and it was a blessing to have my feet on solid ground. Ron stepped off the ship and immediately got land sick. He swayed back and forth with an upset stomach. I felt so awful for him. I had lost ten pounds on the trip and did not want him to go through that horrible feeling too. After all, he was going to be on land a lot longer than I was on the ship.

It was all so hectic for me as an immigrant in a foreign country. However, it was lovely to have a familiar face greet us upon arrival. "Uncle" Ben, a lawyer and longtime friend of Mum's, was there with open arms. Unfortunately, Uncle Ben had just left his briefcase in the taxi on his way to the port. While my husband took care of the baggage, Uncle Ben took me on a chase across the island to retrieve his briefcase. He managed to commandeer an ice cream truck when he bribed the driver to "follow that cab." We did. He got his briefcase back. We laughed about the fact that I had only been in America for ten minutes and had already raced around in an ice cream truck like in some action-adventure movie.

We were also welcomed by a cousin of my dad, Michael Chenagle. He lived and worked in Manhattan and graciously checked to see that we were comfortable in our hotel, and he took us to dinner. What a darling man he was. He was an actor in the Yiddish theater and had appeared in a few Hollywood films. He was a delight, and I was comforted to be in the presence of family.

We spent one night in New York City and then we flew to Kansas City where Ron's family resided. When we made our descent to the airfield, I felt quite ill and knew it was not travel sickness this time, it was pure nerves. For the first time, I would meet my new in-laws.

I started to panic as we drove to Gladstone, which was about twenty miles from Kansas City. We kept going farther into the countryside with fewer buildings in sight. Farmland was all I could see for miles. I suddenly felt trapped and very alone. I wanted to leave and run back home to London immediately. I did not understand why leaving the city environment made me feel so unsettled. The last time I had lived in the countryside was during wartime and these memories evoked sadness and fear. There were certain sounds and sights that were triggers. I was terrified of hearing police sirens as they mimicked the air raid warnings in London. When car dealerships held a grand car sale and displayed searchlights that sliced up the night sky, I clearly remembered being raided by the Germans at night. Some toxic smoke odors also tended to take my mind to these horrors from my past. Despite my anxiety, onward we drove, and we soon arrived in Gladstone.

Ron's family, the Tarwaters, put my fears to rest with their kind, warm, and welcoming ways. Ron's younger siblings were adorable. His teenage sister, Virginia-Jean, quickly became a confidante. His mother, Bertha, was very loving and maternal toward me. Ron's father, Doc, was the most caring of all. Doc, whose given name was also Ron, would sit with me and hold my hand while I cried from homesickness. His years in World War II in the Pacific taught him the terrible feeling of missing home and family. He related to my feelings of being so homesick. He was severely wounded in the Philippines and spent over a year in hospital while they created a synthetic stomach for him. He suffered terribly with stomach upsets when he ate things that did not work in the prosthetic stomach. He also suffered from debilitating migraine headaches for days at a time likely from PTSD. My heart went out to him.

Doc was a man who lovingly teased me. He liked to take advantage of the fact that I didn't know many American slang phrases and local idioms. He once took me to the local town bakery and asked me to go in and get a dozen "bull chips." I had no clue what kind of chips they were, and the people at the counter were giggling when they looked through the window and saw who had set me up for this joke. I returned with these awful looking brown baked goods. They tasted delicious, thankfully not at all what they were named for. In the car Doc told me what bull chips were, we both laughed for the whole car ride home. I never looked at cow dung the same after that.

Halloween came around shortly after we arrived. Ron's family retrieved an old costume for me to wear that belonged to his little brother, David. It was a full-body, head-to-toe costume of a lion. We all got dressed up for trick-or-treat, which I had never heard of. Dressed as a lion, I was introduced as Ron's new wife to all the countryside neighbors. The costume completely obscured my face, so I had to be reintroduced to them on the next occasion we met. We had many laughs about my first American Halloween and my sweet tooth was more than satisfied.

After our month-long stay in Gladstone, Ron had to return to duty at Travis Air Force Base in Fairfield, California. It was located between San Francisco and Sacramento. Prior to our departure, we celebrated our first anniversary. The entire Tarwater crew came to Doc and Bertha's home for our send off. It was quite a large gathering, and we enjoyed a huge family cookout. The clan embraced me with much love and beautiful gifts. I was so grateful to be a part of this loving American family. It was exactly what I had wanted.

We headed out for the long, 1,800-mile drive to the California base. Our newly bought, second-hand DeSoto convertible was loaded to the hilt with luggage and wedding gifts for our trip out West. My anxieties about the countryside assuaged, in large part, because of Doc's kindness and understanding. A new excitement engulfed me as we drove through the beautiful United States. This was the country that I had longed to see since I was a little girl. My dreams were becoming a reality. There was something cathartic about leaving the wartime memories so far away across the Atlantic Ocean.

We drove through Kansas, Nebraska, and then Wyoming. In Wyoming, I saw my very first herd of wild horses running freely across the hills. The sight of those majestic animals was breathtaking. I attended my first rodeo show and it mirrored the movies, although noisier, smellier, and all too violent. It was unbearable to see the animals being "tamed" by the cowboys. I was unaware of the ending, until the trapped defenseless bull was exhausted and brutally killed by the "heroic" matador. It was the first and last rodeo I ever attended.

Our drive through the desert on the outskirts of Salt Lake City was an unusual experience. We were unaware at the time, but we had driven past the Dugway Proving Grounds in Tooele County where the Army placed training targets in the sand for bombing squads to hit while flying over. The explosions hit quite close to the highway on which we traveled and we felt quite unsettled driving through their target practice. I was downright scared. The sight and sound of these detonations resulted in all too real flashbacks. Once again, I was reminded of wartime in England, which continued to haunt me.

When we got to Reno, Nevada, we found a sleepy little town in the desert with casinos on the single main street. It was 1955, three weeks before my twenty-first birthday, so I was barred from entering a casino. Neither Ron nor I had ever experienced gambling or a casino. He had just turned 21 and went inside to try his hand at this new form of entertainment. I watched through the lobby windows. The idea of gambling was exciting, but unfortunately Ron lost more than we could afford. After that, we slept each night in the car and lived on bouillon cubes and hot dogs for days. Thank goodness we were in love. By the time we got to California, we were exhausted and broke.

We arrived at Travis Air Force base with no money to find a place to live. Ron went to the base and took out a loan to pay for one month's rent deposit. He also borrowed bedding, cutlery, pots, and pans. We found a nice one-bedroom flat off base certainly adequate for two people. It was completely furnished.

There were many young newlyweds in the same complex and in the same financial boat as we were. Our apartment community shared everything and spent each evening together as we played cards and talked about our homes and families. No one could afford to go out and do anything too expensive. However, one evening we treated ourselves and went to Chinatown in San Francisco for a wonderful dinner. As we headed toward San Francisco, I was most excited to see the Golden Gate Bridge for the first time. However, the fog was so dense that we drove quite blindly over the bridge and could barely see the road directly in front of us. It was reminiscent of the London fog. When we returned home that evening it was too dark to enjoy the view. I knew there would be other chances to see the magnificent structure.

Within my first week at the base, I was disappointed to discover that to get a job for myself was most unlikely. Once interviewers knew I was the wife of a serviceman, they deduced that my working life was to be short in California. For them, there was no use to train someone who would likely leave in three months or less. I never found a job during our stay there.

The day Ron got out of the Air Force was one of great joy for him. By late 1955, he had served four years. He came home and stripped off his uniform. He neatly packed it away as it had served him well. We said farewell to our new friends and returned to our Missouri family, ready for a new adventure.

SHOW ME

Back in Missouri, Doc had started a new business. In the cellar of his home, Ron's dad had a large printing press, a linotype and other machinery necessary to run a weekly newspaper. It all quite fascinated me. The newspaper was new to their countryside area. Ron was excited to help his father get the newspaper off the ground. To get it known and recognized, Ron acquired advertising from local stores and businesses. Each week when the paper was hot off the press, Ron, his siblings, and I jumped into the bed of the pickup truck while Doc drove us all around the rural countryside. We delivered free papers to every farm in the region. We tossed the newspapers onto residents' lawns. After several weeks and a great reception, people began to purchase the paper and ordered subscriptions. Thus, The Gladstone News was born.

Ron became the editor, wrote most of the articles and sold advertising space. He also set type and helped to run the printing press. His mom, Bertha, did all of the bookkeeping and she was busy morning, noon, and night as she tended to both the business and the family with never a complaint. After Doc purchased all the supplies, made loan payments on the equipment, and paid a union man his wages to do the linotype work, there was little left to pay themselves. Unfortunately, Ron did not get paid for a long time. We felt it.

We found a little cabin that had once been a chicken coop. This became our first real home together in America. It had one small bedroom, a living room, a bathroom, a kitchen sink, and a stove which was all we needed to create a lovely little nest. The low, sloping coop style roof meant that the ceiling was just high enough to allow us to stand, but only if we were under the peak. We placed our couch under the lower side of the slope so that we could sit down and would not bump our heads. We adopted a playful little Corgi in homage to Queen Elizabeth. We named this fawn and white fearless Pembroke Bess. She was a bright little devil. We came home from work one day to find that Bess had taken the end of the toilet paper roll from the bathroom and ran from room to room with it until the roll ran out. Oh, what fun she had in our absence.

We rented the cabin from the farm owners who lived in the big house just behind us. One Sunday, the farmer was painting the exterior of his house. He had all his paint pots lined along the tarpaulin, which was spread out across the lawn. He was balanced on a ladder as he carefully painted the side of his house. Bess had a great time as she slowly and deliberately hauled the corner of the tarp across the lawn. All the paint pots rattled. I watched from my window as the farmer descended the ladder to dip his paintbrush in a pot, and there was no pot to be found. When I saw his astonishment, I went outside and meekly confessed what had happened to his paint. Thank goodness he was a good-natured man and appreciated the humor of the situation. Bess was a master at making us laugh, until she was not. Bess also managed to kill the same farmer's chickens and that was not so funny.

Cooking was not my best talent, so when I finally invited my in-laws over for dinner at the chicken coop, I was extremely nervous. Doc said he would like an English shepherd's pie with apple pie for dessert. Everything looked wonderful, and I was proud to present my home cooked meal. As I served the main course, it came out of the Pyrex dish like a lump of fired clay, shiny, hard, and totally inedible. It had to be dumped in the garbage. To add insult to injury, the shepherd's pie made a huge thump as it hit the bottom of the can. Now the fine-looking apple pie became the main course. My father-in-law kindly said it smelled divine as I brought it to the table with great care. Doc could not wait to taste this apple sensation. I warned him that it was ridiculously hot as it had just left the oven. He took the first bite. His expression was one of a man with his mouth on fire. I had never used cinnamon before, and accidentally grabbed the red pepper. I sprinkled it carefully over the pie. That, too, went into the garbage can. My cooking never really improved and continued to be the butt of many family jokes.

Within weeks I found a job in North Kansas City where I typed and did simple bookkeeping. I was terrible at figures but somehow managed to stay employed. A few months after I started the job, I joyfully discovered I was pregnant. We were thrilled to welcome our first child and become a family of three. Two and a half months later, I suffered a miscarriage while at work. Ron's mother, Bertha, came to take me home. It was a horrible blow, and I was terribly upset to lose the baby. Bertha assured me there would be other pregnancies and that life would go on. She was right.

After the miscarriage, my homesickness returned and all I wanted to do was go home to my family. Doc so graciously helped collect a small amount of money from family and friends to help me to afford a trip home. My wages and Doc's generous contribution allowed me to travel by ship back to England to visit my family. I had mixed emotions when I left as Ron and I had never been apart since we got married, but it felt vital for me to make the trip.

I traveled by train to New York City to board the ship that would sail me to England. I felt nauseous for nearly twelve hundred miles and was sick for the entire journey. I met a lovely couple on the train who took pity on me. The young woman, Mary, was from the Bronx and her husband, Jules, was a new immigrant from Belgium. They understood my homesickness and my dilemma to leave my husband while I traveled home alone to England. I was so ill that I forgot to pick up my luggage when we arrived at Grand Central Station in New York. The couple took things into their own hands and invited me back to their apartment after they gathered all my suitcases. Grateful, I spent the night at their flat.

I had to set sail early the next morning. Mary and Jules called a taxi and safely escorted me to the Queen Mary to see me off. How unbelievably kind the couple was. They took in a total stranger and showed me such compassion. They even mailed me a jacket I had forgotten at the flat as I had given them my address in hopes we would keep up a correspondence. I did not know how to repay such generous hearts.

NOT SO MERRY OLD ENGLAND

The conditions back at home in England, at least for the people who were closest to me, was nothing short of terrible. I heard from my siblings that my parents weren't speaking to each other. I wanted to see the situation firsthand. I had written to tell Mum I was on my way home and that my ship would dock at Southampton. Mum was there to greet me and I feasted my eyes at the sight of this absolutely magnificent woman. The love just flowed out of her and into me. I felt my soul healing already. Mum drove me home, her presence was nurturing. Upon arriving home, however, my sister Gloria and brother Brian passed messages between our parents even when they were in the same room. Dad was irrationally strict about what groceries Mum could purchase. Groceries were delivered to the house where Dad checked each item and sent back anything that he had not approved. He was completely controlling and very stingy with money, even when it came to necessities. There were few light bulbs in the house that worked because Dad claimed it was a waste of money to have more than one light on in each room. It was terrible for Gloria and Brian to live under such strain. Mum found it nearly intolerable.

I stayed at home for four weeks and got a temporary job to pay my fare back to the States. During that time, I tried to help resolve some tense issues within my family. I was always favored by my dad and sometimes I was the only one who could get through to him. We thought it was best for him to move to America and to start anew. He had a brother who resided in Illinois and a few other family members that had moved abroad. My parents put our house on the market and with the forthcoming money from the sale, Dad planned to move to Elgin, Illinois to live with his brother, Syd. Dad had the promise of a job as a furrier, where he would create and repair fur garments, which was right up his alley. Mum wanted to move to New York City, a dream of hers. She also felt the need to start anew, but Dad argued, "America is not big enough to hold us both."

Brian was not 16-years-old at the time and needed both parents' signatures on a release form that would allow him to leave England and go to America.

Dad refused to sign the papers. He did not want Mum and the children to follow him. I tried repeatedly to talk with Dad about signing the papers for Brian. One night, I stayed up until two in the morning to try to convince him. I assured him that where he was headed in Illinois was more than a thousand miles from where Mum and the children were planning to live in New York City. I begged him to reconsider. Finally, he begrudgingly signed the forms. For this I was happy to have made the journey.

The house sold after I left England and Dad left immediately for Elgin. Until they could arrange the paperwork to leave England themselves, Mum, Brian, and Gloria stayed at a friend's house. They would eventually move to New York when all the details were settled. I was ecstatic.

ANOTHER LIFE

I traveled on the grand and beautiful ship The Queen Elizabeth during my journey back to America. In the evenings, the orchestra played in the grand ballroom and my feet were longing to dance, but I had no partner. One evening, a handsome young man in an American Army uniform approached me. He sweetly bowed down and gently held my hand as he asked me to dance with him. I replied, "Yes," before effortlessly gliding onto the dance floor. Never in my life had I quite literally been swept off my feet as I was that first dance with Luc and everyone after. We danced the entire evening. I can recall the amazing feeling of unity in every step. The dance floor emptied, and we were alone moving so naturally that one would have thought the young serviceman and I had danced together for years. Everyone surrounded us and watched, waiting for a break in our steps, expecting a mistake, which never came. I followed him precisely.

The following evening, the two of us danced every step from exotic tangos and romantic waltzes to ballroom foxtrots and sensual rumbas. I did not understand how I was able to follow Luc so accurately. As the evening ended, he revealed that although he was from Belgium, he was in the United States Army on their competition dance team traveling the world. He had won international awards for the Army Dance Team, which to some degree explained the reason dancing with him seemed so effortless. He was a professional and knew how to lead. He confessed that in all his years dancing, he had never met a partner who could follow him as I did. Our chemistry was undeniable.

Luc asked me if there was any possibility that I would join him during his jaunts around the world to dance competitively. With some practice together he believed we could win many competitions. I was speechless. A dream of a lifetime was being offered to me and I was dumbfounded.

However, facts had to be faced. I told him I was married to a wonderful young man who was newly out of the Air Force, and I was on my way back to Missouri to continue our lives together. He admitted to me that his pregnant wife was in his cabin and not well enough to leave, which is why he was alone every evening. I explained to him that he had offered me an opportunity nearly too difficult to refuse. However, for me to leave my husband to follow that dream was unimaginable and unrealistic. I was truly flattered. For a moment, anyway, it was amusing to fantasize about an exotic alternate life for myself.

LEAVING MISSOURI

Within a year, our lawyer friend, Uncle Ben, managed to get Mum, Gloria, and Brian to America. He helped them settle in an apartment in Fort Lee, New Jersey. Mum got a secretarial job at a publishing firm in Bergen County, New Jersey. Gloria found work in New York City in the garment district. Brian had been out of school for over a year in England and had worked as an apprentice at an accounting firm. However, he was too young to finish school in America, so he attended high school for another year until he graduated American style. It was comforting to have them in America. Even so, they were a thousand miles away and I longed to see them.

Things got tougher for Ron and me in Missouri. Although I worked, Ron had been without pay for quite some time working with his father at the newspaper. The heat in Missouri was stifling and it was uncomfortable without air-conditioning in our cabin. In addition, my escalating animosity towards racism was becoming a point of friction.

On my way to work one morning via the local bus, I made my way to the back and took a seat. The bus driver demanded, "Move to the front part of the bus. The back is for niggers only."

I was shocked and furious. I refused to move, so the driver refused to drive the bus. I would not compromise my principles. The other passengers jeered, held up their fists, and made a lot of noise about my decision. Apparently, I was the problem. They would be late for work because of me. Finally, I had to concede and move to a front seat, or we would not be able to travel anywhere. The bus driver was stern in his conviction. In the rear of the bus, the black riders looked terribly uncomfortable. The whole situation made me heartsick. Having stones thrown at me on the way to the Jewish school when I was a girl had made me particularly sensitive to prejudice. I can vividly remember the feelings of hatred toward me and my family. My intentions of solidarity with the people who were forced to ride in the back of the bus were fruitless.

One morning we found a large funeral wreath sitting on our doorstep. We believe it was placed there by the local police. It was a clear message to us that Ron should quiet his liberal opinions. This ominous threat frightened us. We felt resistance from the community and from within Ron's family as well. They did not want trouble at their doorstep, understandably. At one dinner with his parents, Ron and I told them about how the press works in England, with true freedom of speech. Doc labeled us Communists. The government aiding their people with socialized healthcare, public transportation, or any programs in which the government was involved he considered linked to Communism. I had always believed there was freedom of speech in America, but that was not completely true at that time. The McCarthy Era investigations were the headlines, and no one dared open their mouths for fear they would be labeled a Communist and blacklisted. There was heightened political repression of people who leaned left-wing. Ron felt it was time to move on. I concurred.

Although he had been happy when he completed his service, Ron signed up for the Air Force and asked to be posted in England. We felt that our political views were more closely aligned with those of Great Britain. After we left Kansas City, Ron headed to Andrews Air Force Base in Maryland to the Strategic Air Command and, thankfully, was assigned to England as he had requested. I decided to visit Fort Lee to stay with my family as we couldn't afford to ship me home at that point. I found a job where I could earn enough for my fare to England, this was becoming the norm. I was ecstatic about being with my family, although I knew it was only for a short time. Shortly after Ron left for England, I discovered that I was pregnant once again.

Until I could join Ron in England, I got a job as a teletypist in Fort Lee, New Jersey. I encouraged Gloria to come and work with me so that we could be together for as long as I was in the States. The group I worked with was wonderful. At our facility there was a terrific warehouse crew. They lived in the upper story of the factory instead of paying for motel rooms or apartments.

This is where I met Raymond Polett who worked in the warehouse. He was tall, handsome, had a quick wit and great sense of humor. He took this job while he was waiting to start as a cadet in the police academy. I suggested to Gloria to quit her job in the garment district so she could work with me and meet this gorgeous man. That's exactly what she did. It was love at first sight for Gloria and she confided to me that if she could get just one date with Raymond, her life would be so sweet that she would give up her favorite jelly doughnuts.

We had a lot of fun with Ray. Our friendship grew and he was kind enough to pick us both up for work in his little Volkswagen Beetle each day at the crack of dawn. One very snowy morning, Gloria stayed home sick, and I went downstairs alone to catch my ride with Ray. There were about ten steps down to the driveway, but they were so heavily covered in snow that the steps had all but disappeared. Ray waited by the car as I stepped toward him and vanished into the snowbank right up to my neck. My coat was spread out all around me on top of the snow and Ray came to rescue me. He grabbed me by the collar of my coat and hauled me out as I howled with laughter. From the fourth-floor window, Gloria giggled as she watched the entire bungle.

In 1957, I left Fort Lee and returned to England to reunite with Ron. My darling mother, brother, and sister came to the ship to see me off and I waved goodbye as they stood on the dock. My tears blinded me, and I could barely walk to my cabin. At the top of a flight of stairs, my shoe heel caught in the hem of my coat, and I tumbled down the entire flight of stairs. No one saw me, but I felt more embarrassed than hurt. I went straight to my cabin.

The Liberté was a wonderful old ship that had been confiscated during the war from the French by the Germans to be used as transport for their soldiers. The French took it back after the war and lovingly restored it to its former glory. As this ship was bound for France, most of the people on board were European and from France. Many passengers and crew spoke other languages. Fortunately, among the group of Europeans seated at my dining table was one elderly French lady who spoke English quite fluently. She heard me order the most abominable meal combinations, and thereafter helped me order my food. I was fascinated seeing bottles of both red and white wines on each table to accompany the fare. Everyone, including the children, drank wine with their meals as if it were water. I stuck to water.

Not surprisingly, a dense fog greeted *The Liberté* as we arrived in Plymouth, England. Only a few passengers out of the many hundreds on board needed to disembark from the ship. The captain decided not to dock this large vessel as it was too dangerous in the fog. At five o'clock in the morning, a fishing trawler sidled up to the ship to take us to port. The lovely friends I made were awake at that early hour to hug me goodbye. I was to climb down the rope ladder of a ship approximately four stories high and wearing high- heeled shoes, no less. I was scared that I would plunge into the ocean, yet there was no other choice than to climb or continue to France. I gingerly descended and arrived safely on the trawler.

I was amazed as I neared the dock and saw Ron's loving face and his arms reaching out to embrace me. I had my own wonderful surprise for him when I joyfully divulged that I was pregnant. I did not write to tell him because I knew he would get much more pleasure from the big news by sharing it personally.

We had no home yet, so Ron booked us into a bed and breakfast in Uxbridge, outside of London. A few days later, I awoke feeling awful and found, to my horror, that I was hemorrhaging badly. Ron had left for the base, and we had no phone in our room. I crawled to the door of our room and shouted for help. I was carried out on a stretcher to an ambulance and rushed to hospital.

While in hospital Ivor, Freda, Stan, and Maurice visited me. Doctors tried an unusual method to try to save the baby. I had to lie on my stomach tilted forward and face down. I could not see my sweet visitor's lovely faces while we were having a conversation. It was a strange way to greet them all after so many years apart. They had traveled nearly three hours to see me and their support helped me through another difficult time. The doctors thought they would be able to save the baby this time, but, sadly, such was not the case. For the second time, I lost the child I had carried, but remembered my mother-in-law, Bertha's encouraging words and trusted that everything would be okay.

The first letter I received upon returning to England was from Gloria. It read, in part, "Guess what? I've given up jelly doughnuts."

Not long after, Gloria and Ray were married. Considering Dad did not want to have any involvement with our family, Uncle Bob Lahr, the cousin of actor Burt Lahr, who played the "Cowardly Lion" in The Wizard of Oz, gave her away. Bob was a dear friend of my Mum whom we had met in Somerset during the war. He was one of the American Airmen who so kindly gave us candy and comic books when we were children. Bob was dear to our hearts, and we were forever grateful to him for comforting us in the war. We remained friends with Uncle Bob until his passing in 2004. Sometimes, one's family are those we choose rather than those we are given.

We found a little flat in a sweet lady's private home. We lived there until Ron found a lovely cottage to rent. Soon after our move, Bertha and Ron's seven-year-old brother, David, came to visit us in England. It was a grand adventure for them as neither had previously left Missouri nor flown on an airplane. We enjoyed taking them on tours of historic London. We saw the Horse Guards Parade, Buckingham Palace, and the Prime Minister's home at 10 Downing Street. It was incredible luck when just as we arrived, Winston Churchill exited his home and got into his limousine along with his plump bulldog, Dodo. He proudly puffed on his famous cigar and waved kindly at the crowd.

A month after Ron's mother and brother returned to America, I discovered I was pregnant for the third time. I was terrified that this pregnancy would end as the first two did.

My pregnancy was difficult, and I suffered unceasingly from morning sickness. The pregnancy went full term. When I finally went into labor, I was admitted to the Hammersmith Hospital in London. In my admission papers, they asked my religious preference. I said I would like a visit from a rabbi as I was of Jewish heritage. Ironically, the delivery doctor was German and, I assume because she still held prejudice left over from the war, she behaved with disdain towards me.

I had been bedridden with dysentery for two weeks prior to the birth and was vomiting throughout the entire delivery. The doctor continually screamed, "Stop it!" Of course, I had no control over my illness. She refused to call for a nurse or any aid. My husband wasn't allowed in the delivery room, so Ron knew nothing of what took place. Once again, I felt alone and persecuted.

The labor was ultimately successful and quite a relief. I had a beautiful, healthy baby boy. Sadly, after the birth, I was not allowed to see or hold my newborn son Scott, named for Scotland. For three days, due to dysentery, I was separated from Scott. I worried that I didn't really have a baby and that something tragic had happened to him. One day a kind nurse came to the window of my hospital room and held Scott up for me to see from head to toe. What a blessing that nurse gave me.

HARD TIMES

After Scott was born in May of 1959, our little family moved to a lovely bungalow in the countryside. It was built at the end of the runway at Heathrow Airport. Scott was a bonnie child and smiled at everyone. He had such a sunny nature.

When Scott was a year old, Ron started to feel the effects of the stress resulting from his work with the Strategic Air Command. Our lives were not our own anymore. He was called in at all hours of the day and night for various exercises due to panic warnings from the USSR. In 1960, there was constant fear that Russia would launch a nuclear attack on the United States and their ally, Great Britain.

We were not permitted to travel beyond a 30-mile radius from our home without permission from the base commander. When seeing a movie, we were required to report what part of the theater we would be seated. Ron lamented this lack of freedom, and it began to take its toll on our marriage.

I was equally as stressed because I could see how his situation affected him. I was also struggling as I tried to raise a baby with no outside help or counsel. I had rarely held a baby before becoming a mother. Having limited resources and knowledge of caring for a newborn, I was scared that I would do something wrong. My nearest friends and relatives lived over two hours away by public transportation. Had my family or friends lived nearby, I would have felt far more confident.

One evening, Ron was called back to the base immediately after arriving home from work. He worked on a United States Air Force magazine alongside a British civilian who did the printing. The printer had an attractive seventeen-year-old daughter who came to the base with him. After meeting his co-worker's daughter, Ron became immediately infatuated by her. Thus, I would take yet another unfortunate turn and would change our lives forever.

Ron and the young woman became romantically involved, which unearthed stress and unhappiness for both of us. He began to treat me platonically. I was his confidant as he shared his woes regarding the young girl. I cried constantly, I was deeply depressed and barely ate. I found it difficult to properly take care of Scott in my terrible state of mind. My depression became severe. Ron was the main cause so he could not help me pass through it.

The only people who knew of our marriage troubles were my two closest friends, Stan and Maurice. I could not bear to tell other friends and relatives. Most had believed our marriage to be a fairytale. We were known as a stable and loving couple. The addition of our beautiful baby boy seemed to complete the perfect picture. Although I remained deeply in love with Ron, the image we reflected was not a reality. Our marriage was, in fact, broken and I felt isolated and ashamed.

Given the circumstances, I decided to leave England and Ron. I planned to return to the United States with Scott to be near my Mum and siblings. I needed their loving support. Maurice and Stan begged me to stay in England. They offered their spare bedroom to Scott and I in hopes the affair would blow over. Ron meant so much to me. I knew if I stayed, even if we lived apart, I would run to him if ever he asked. I was quite firm in my decision to go.

The choices people make under duress are not always the best ones, but I never regretted that decision.

 I wrote to Mum in New Jersey and asked if she could borrow some money to pay for our fares, once again. Shortly after, I had the ticket money in-hand and booked a USAF flight with many other young mothers with children who were also headed back to the United States. There were over a hundred other children on the flight. Propeller planes used in 1960 to transport the families of the airmen were much slower than modern jets. It took us twelve hours to fly from London to New York.

Scott was the most adorable baby, and I was truly grateful that he was such an angel on that flight. It felt as though he sensed that my heart was being tugged away from me as we traveled further away from England and his father. Scott laughed and giggled at the other children on the plane. He suckled his warm bottle and settled down to sleep on my lap for much of the flight. He was 14-months-old, bald, plump, and was not yet walking. I weighed 78-pounds due to my lack of nutrition and severe depression. I had not been eating properly and Scott was quite a heavy lump for me to carry, but I was determined to start anew.

Upon our arrival in the States, Mum and my brother, Brian, were there to greet us. Their love abounded, which immediately began my healing process. I shared with Mum that my marriage was in trouble, and I needed to live in New York without Ron. She consoled me and assured me that we would be okay. She was overjoyed to meet her first grandchild. I knew my decision to leave was the right one.

Gloria, her husband Ray, and their darling new baby, Bob, were my saving grace. I decided to live in Norwich, New York, where Gloria and Ray lived. By that time, Ray worked as a New York State Trooper and Gloria stayed home with their son. Gloria would watch Scott so I could get a day job. They owned a trailer home and helped me get a bank loan for a trailer right next door to them. The trailer park was very small with only six trailers. Each home had its own level on the hill with a nice yard. Gloria and Ray were essentially one step away.

I secured a job as a teletypist with the Norwich Pharmaceuticals Company, which, for all intents and purposes, owned the town of Norwich. I did not yet know how to drive, so a kind neighbor drove me to work each day. Ray or a neighbor would drive Gloria and I to get groceries. I had what I needed to rebuild my life and begin to heal my heart.

At Norwich Pharmaceuticals, I liked the work itself, but grew to dislike the company and the people who worked there. They were not the kindest or easiest to get along with. The woman I worked for was an alcoholic and was often drunk by nine in the morning. It was almost impossible to work for her as she was incoherent most of the day. In her lucid moments, which were few, we got along great. However, most of the time she threw pens, pencils, paper clips, and stationary at me from behind to gain my attention. Her behavior was so erratic that the women in the typing pool sat glued to their chairs in disbelief. Many people left that job due to her abuse, but I did not have the luxury of being able to quit. This was the only big company in town. The time I spent there seemed never ending and unyielding. However, it paid the bills and put food on our table.

I dated on occasion, but my heart was not in it. No one could measure up to Ron. I was still so in love with him despite his unfaithfulness. I could not bear that Scott did not have his loving father to help raise him.

Eventually, Gloria and Ray were able to afford a small house on the outskirts of town and they moved. We were no longer neighbors, so I needed to find another babysitter. Two or three different people took care of Scott at one time or another. I went to work each day worried about how they would treat my little boy and it tore at my heart. I often went into the ladies' room to cry. I thought of my Mum during the evacuation of London during World War II. Her anguish must have tormented her.

The weather in upstate New York was horrific when the season changed to winter. The temperature could drop as low as forty degrees below zero. It was said that it was sometimes colder than it was in Alaska. I left my winter clothes in England as we were allowed one suitcase on the plane. My suitcases were filled with Scott's baby clothes; I had no room for bulky sweaters. To keep warm was a major undertaking for me when I waited for my ride at the bottom of the hill at the trailer park. At work on those cold mornings, I had to run warm water over my blue hands before I was able to sit down and type.

A year later, the company cut back to only one teletypist. I happily kept my position as others were let go. Their first computer was delivered at Norwich Pharmaceuticals that year. It was housed in the room adjacent to my office. The computer was so huge it filled an entire 12'x12' room. The temperature had to remain level day and night. No one could enter without permission to keep the temperature constant. Next to my desk they placed a huge machine that spewed out three-by-eight-inch cards with holes in them. The holes were codes sent by the gigantic computer in the next room. I was required to read them between my teletyping work. Computers were remarkably different from what they have become today.

The population in Norwich was so small and the main entertainment was gossip. I went to our 1890's themed company picnic one summer where we were to dress in period clothing. One friend found her grandmother's old swimming costume. She was too big to fit into the tiny suit. She offered it to me, and I obliged as I had nothing else to wear. Prior to the start of the picnic a photographer mingled and shot photos of all the guests that were dressed in period garb. I was shocked when I heard my name announced over the loudspeaker as "Queen of the Day." I was led to a golf cart and driven around the grounds dressed in the black, long, very old-fashioned swimsuit. It covered me from head to toe. I also wore a white, cotton, lace-edged hat. I was awarded a huge single sunflower. I not only looked like an idiot, I felt like one as well.

A man who also worked at the large company kindly gave me a lift to the picnic. He was very generous to let me ride with him after hearing the disheartening gossip about me in my outfit. I left the event early to go home and start the weekend with Scott. The same gentleman dropped me off at my house and then he went straight home. By Monday morning both of our names were mud. Horrid rumors were created about the two of us. The gossip was disgusting and malicious. I worried about him because he had his wife to consider. Thankfully, she knew the small-town minds well enough to understand their bitterness and strong tendencies to gossip. She and her husband were from South America and were also struggling to adjust to this tiny company town.

REUNITED

After two lonely years apart from Ron, he finally returned to the United States. The year was 1962 when he left the Air Force and returned to Kansas City. He asked me to visit so his parents could meet their first little grandson. He also wanted to see how Scott had grown and wanted to make a connection with his young son. Scott and I flew from Syracuse to Missouri. Our visit was somewhat estranged. I wanted to be with Ron, but not if the young woman was still in the picture.

Shortly thereafter, Ron sent for her in England to come to Missouri. Based on Ron's account, when she descended the steps of the plane, he said that he wondered to himself, "What the devil am I doing?"

Ron claimed he had lost feelings for her and wanted to get out of the situation immediately. She had a sister in Canada, so Ron bought her a ticket and sent her north. He asked if he could visit Scott and I in Norwich. I was very hesitant, but we made the practical decision to try again to work things out together for Scott's sake . . . and for mine. Love is both a powerful force and, often, a blind one too.

The three of us continued to live in Norwich and Ron became editor of a local newspaper, The Norwich Sun. Although it was not easy, I believed Ron and I stood a better chance to make things work if we were together and shared the burdens and joys of life instead of trying to do so apart. We found a stone house, a converted barn, in the countryside. The house had stone walls, inside and out, and huge, flat, stone floors, with a cozy fireplace. We loved it. I was both anxious and excited for this fresh start together.

The windows in the bedroom had a peculiar six-inch board nailed to the front of the sill to prevent things from falling onto the floor. One night when we were sound asleep, loud bolts of lightning cracked in the dark skies. My treasured collection of china statues jumped up over the shelf barrier and crashed to the stone floor. Not one remained whole. We were shocked.

We discussed this odd phenomenon with the owners of the stone house. They had a most unusual response to our story. Many years ago, the cow barn had caught fire at night during a violent storm. Every cow died while desperately struggling to exit the burning barn. Thereafter, on stormy nights, it seemed, poltergeists continued to exhibit their desperation and knocked over anything on the windowsill next to where they perished. We understood why the unusual piece of wood was installed. According to the property owners, the previous renters had experienced similar phenomena during storms.

As time moved forward, we faced many burdens from our jobs, which primarily hinged on politics and freedom of the press. We observed the same resistance to freedom of the press that we experienced in Missouri when Ron was the newspaper editor of The Gladstone News in 1955. Again, Ron and I did not often agree with our community's politics. Norwich Pharmaceuticals was firmly entrenched in conservative politics as was The Norwich Sun. When Democrats tried to place advertisements during the election year, they were routinely rejected. Ron was thoroughly appalled and, therefore, refused advertisements from any political party. He would not back down. Inevitably, Ron was terminated by the paper. I had great admiration for Ron and when he lost his job, I was proud of him for standing by his beliefs. He wasn't going to beg to keep his job if it meant he had to acquiesce to the biased company culture.

When Robert Kennedy visited the town, we went to meet him at the tiny airfield. We traveled two cars behind him in a long cavalcade of handsome limousines along Main Street. We and the Catholic nuns were among the few in town permitted to drive so near to The United States Attorney General. Kennedy drew a big crowd, and we were among the few who would admit to being Democrats.

After job hunting for the best fit, Ron accepted a job in Puerto Rico with The San Juan Star. He found it hard to leave his family in New York, but he left to see what the job and lifestyle would be for us and our young son. Housing in Puerto Rico was not the easiest or safest place to find for three non-Spanish speaking people. School options were limited, which was a consideration for our Scott, who would soon start kindergarten. However, Ron chose to stay in Puerto Rico and give it a chance.

On November 22, 1963, the nation experienced a tragedy beyond words, President John F. Kennedy's untimely assassination. Ron was at work early that morning and was the first to see the message come over the teletype in his office. He created the shocking and sad headline for The San Juan Star in tears that morning.

Early in1964, Ron had decided that Puerto Rico would not be the best choice to raise our son, so he left Puerto Rico. As beautiful as Puerto Rico was, he had seen enough to know that he was not confident raising his family there and he returned to New York.

Once again, Gloria and Ray came to our aid. We put our few belongings into storage and moved to Lowville, New York, where my sister and brother-in-law had recently bought a beautiful home. The bitter cold weather near the Canadian border was greatly moderated by the love and warmth of family. Gloria and Ray had just welcomed their second beautiful son, Thomas. I learned of my pregnancy with our second child, and we were all elated. We had a place to stay in their home until we could figure out our next step. Young Scott and Bobby got along famously and were forever bonded as best cousins. Ron sent out resumes to find a solid job so he could raise his growing family. He took a low-wage job at the tiny ski hill nearby while I sat tight and played the waiting game for my water to break. Within a few weeks, however, Ron was called to Albany to be interviewed by the New York State Comptroller's Office who had heard of his courageous stand against the biased newspaper reporting in Norwich. Ron's record of integrity and knowledge had impressed Comptroller Arthur Levitt who hired him as a speechwriter and public relations director. It seemed the perfect niche for Ron, and we were thrilled that he had secured a solid job. Albany was a two and a half drive from Lowville. Clearly not a sustainable commute. Ron began the hunt for a new home for our family that was closer to his workplace.

A few weeks after Ron started his job in Albany, Lowville was buried in snow. I went into labor. Ron was in Albany at the New York State Capitol, and I needed to get to the hospital. On more than one occasion, Ray had taken other state trooper's wives who were in labor to the same hospital while their husbands were on-duty. To the staff at Lewis County General Hospital, Ray must have appeared to be a busy man.

All but the last four inches of the antenna on Ray's old Jeep was under the snow. He dug the Jeep out of the snow and rushed me to the hospital. Later that day, our sweet daughter, Erin, was born and Ray was the first to hold her. From that day forward, a special bond between Erin and her Uncle Ray was undeniable. We were blessed to have my sister and Ray to look after Scott until I returned to their house with our beautiful, dainty newborn baby girl.

Meanwhile, Ron had found an apartment in Albany. He had our furniture delivered so that the children and I could move, and we could all be together. There was not yet a telephone in the apartment when I went into labor. When Erin was born, a co-worker from his office drove over to tell him he had just become a father of a little girl. Ron came to see Erin when she was three days old. Nine days later, our family of four moved to Albany.

I was thrilled to be home and I was in love with our new little bundle of joy. We got our phone installed and I was happy to make this new apartment into a beautiful home. However, sometime during that week, I caught a horrendous cold that quickly turned into double pneumonia. Ron had to take precious time from his new job to take care of Erin and Scott while I was admitted for what turned out to be two weeks at St. Peter's Hospital in Albany. I was sick in more ways than one as I could not bear to be away from the children. Erin was only three weeks old, and Scott had just begun first grade in a new school. I was frightened that I would slip into depression. Being away from my loved ones reminded me of the separation from my family as a child during the war. Once again, I struggled against those painful memories that consumed me. All I wanted to do was go home to be with my family. Against the backdrop of my growing depression, I learned of nearly the worst news possible.

Mum had not called to check on me or to ask about Scott and her new granddaughter. This was very unusual and completely out of character. Ron struggled with tears flowing to tell me that Mum had been admitted to New York Presbyterian Hospital simultaneously as I was giving birth to undergo a radical mastectomy. This news was a terrible blow as I had not been aware of my mother's illness. She didn't tell me to protect me during my pregnancy. She felt I did not need the extra stress and worry. It broke my heart that I could not be there to love and support her during this terrible time.

I was too weak to visit her even when I left the hospital. She was receiving chemotherapy and was extremely ill. She rode the subway to work each day as she could not afford to leave her only source of income. Just after I arrived home, she called me from the hairdressers at the hospital. She was able to walk around while hooked up to several tubes and she wanted to get her hair washed and set. She laughed and joked as though she was at a picnic. I do not know where she found her amazing strength and her marvelous outlook on life. This jogged my memory of her positive behavior which she maintained around our family during wartime London. She never showed us her panic or worry, she always remained jovial. My Mum, Rosalie, was a strong, positive force on this earth.

As soon as I was able, I traveled to the Bronx with baby Erin and young Scott to see their Nana. Mum had not met her new granddaughter. Erin immediately was Mum's little princess. Mum loved, diapered, and fed her so that I could rest. Likewise, Scott was her perfect angel. Scott responded to this adulation and worshiped his nana. Mum practiced lots of love and praise and she believed that the rest would take care of itself. Her model of behavior has proved true for me time and time again.

HOME SWEET HOME

After a time living in the Albany apartment, Ron and I found a tiny, ancient, stone house situated high atop a hill out in the countryside 20-miles west of Albany. We asked Dad to loan us two thousand dollars for a down payment to buy our very first home in East Berne, New York. We moved into the house when Erin was two-years-old and Scott was eight. Ron was needed in New York City for a few weeks while his boss was campaigning for another four-year term as state comptroller. Before Ron left for that campaign trip, we moved all the furniture and boxes into the new house. There was so much to do, I hardly knew where I would begin. Ron had our only car, while I was literally in the middle of nowhere and knew no one. If I needed help, I had no family or friends nearby.

As I was busy unpacking, I looked down and saw a mouse scurry along the floor in the living room. I jumped onto the couch yelling and screaming. Scott was my little hunter and chased after the mouse with a broom but could not catch it. I stood on the couch and picked up the phone. I called Gloria and Ray, who offered to drive the 150-miles with their Siamese cat, Yoko, as she was the best mouser in the world. As promised, Ray arrived early the next morning. He left us the fierce mouse hunter and returned home as he had to work. The next day, Yoko the hunter earned her keep. The furry rodent was history. Scott knew I detested mice. Although he did not exactly like them himself, he bravely scooped it up and put it in the garbage.

In 1960's New York, water was at a premium. Near drought conditions resulted in the 26-foot deep well on the property being all but dry. We survived on the water that was delivered by the fire department for a healthy fee. We learned that the dry well had been an artesian well, where water flowed freely for decades. Before the house was built, during the Great Depression, we learned neighbors from all around the countryside came with containers to collect the water.

We purchased the house from an engineer and his family, who had lived there for over ten-years. The engineer, in his great wisdom, decided to blow up dynamite to create a large crater fifty feet away from the well. This would become his bomb shelter. During the late fifties, the fear of a Russian atomic bomb attack in the States was very real. Consequently, when he blew the vast hole in the ground, he blew up the artesian well along with it. By the time we moved into the house, the well was empty save for hundreds of snakes that had made it their home.

A neighbor helped us build a new well. He knew how to divine for water with a V- shaped apple tree branch, which was thoroughly fascinating. He walked over our entire two acres of property. His hands held the two ends of the branch with the "v" of the branch pointed toward the surface of the ground. The stick dipped sharply and pulled strongly when he approached underground spring water. It miraculously pointed to the exact spot where water could be found. Of course, we all had to try out the divining method for ourselves, as it seemed like a magic trick. Erin went first. She was so tiny that the pull of the apple branch tossed her to the ground. Nobody else fell over, but the pull was extremely strong.

Wells are measured by the foot to determine both the depth and the cost, so it was important to find out how far down the water was. In order to measure, my neighbor placed a long skeleton key in his Bible and secured it with a small piece of string. He held the string loosely, so the Bible turned easily of its own accord with no help from the diviner who explained that one turn of the Bible equaled one hundred feet. He let the Bible hang from the string over the spot where it slowly turned three and a half times, which indicated 350 feet down. We added another 20-feet to the 350 to hold more storage once the water was flowing.

Our house did not have a traditional heating system. The old dirt floored cellar housed perhaps the largest furnace in a private home. It had six sides with six four-foot-high filters, and it was fueled by coal. By 1967, coal was becoming a fuel of the past. We had our coal delivered from Pennsylvania. We would bank up the fire at night. By morning, the fire was very low, and the house got extremely cold.

On our first Christmas Eve, we left all the toys and gifts under the tree and went to bed with excited anticipation of the festivities to come. The upstairs of the house had no heat vents, so we needed to get the downstairs rooms hot enough that the heat rose and warmed our bedrooms. We banked the furnace with extra coal so that we had a warm night.

During the night, the fire in the furnace became too intense. The old wooden walls started to overheat. Hot sap oozed through the wooden beams. In the early hours of Christmas morning, we called the fire department. The plastic toy buggy for Erin was closest to the wall and had already melted. There were no flames, but the walls were so hot that the firemen stayed until they cooled hours later. We were grateful that we caught the problem before it turned tragic.

After this dangerous episode, we ordered a proper heating system from Sears. We were relieved that we finally had a safe furnace in the cellar and vents heating the upstairs rooms. No longer did we shovel coal in the middle of the night or come home to a house where we could see our breath.

The old stone house sat atop a steep hill. The only access in winter was by way of a primitive ski lift built by the engineer who previously lived there. The lift consisted of three oil drums welded together like a three-leaf clover, with the middle cut out. In the front of one drum, there was a carved-out section where we stepped up and we filled the other two drums with groceries, laundry, or whatever needed to go up the hill.

To run the lift, someone had to be at the top of the hill where they placed the belt onto the wheels of the engine and pressed the start button to start the lift's slow ascension. To return to the bottom, someone had to take the belt off, so the drums flew down the hill with the force of gravity. There was only the hand brake, located high on the cable, which stopped us at the other end. The cable itself reached about thirty feet in the air, which was as high as the telephone lines. It was frightening and someone always needed to walk up the hill to start the mechanisms. When the technicians from Sears installed our new heating system, it was the dead of winter with snow drifts fifteen feet high lining the driveway. The only way for them to get all the needed equipment to the top of the hill was to put them on the lift, piece by piece. Slowly, the delivery men loaded components.

The ski lift was also a great conversation piece. The delivery men were so fascinated with the whole contraption that they told the Albany newspaper about it. Soon after, the reporter interviewed and photographed us alongside the ski lift and Scott, sledding down the hill to the bottom of the driveway, where he waited for the school bus. A two-page centerfold complete with pictures of our family and our unique method of transportation appeared in the Sunday edition of the newspaper.

We used this cumbersome contraption for quite a while until my brother, Brian, came to visit with his buddy from New Jersey for a weekend. They had the brilliant idea to wire the motor so it could run both ways. Now there was no need to remove the belt when going down the hill. Instead, we turned on the motor from either the top or the bottom of the hill. For a couple of months, Brian's modification worked wonderfully.

One bitterly cold night when Ron arrived home from work, he stepped into the barrel, turned on the motor, and got halfway up the hill when the motor failed. The ski lift would not move in either direction. He hung in mid-air in the barrel as it swayed to and fro in the biting wind. He shouted for me to try to turn the motor on so that he could ascend the rest of the way up. It was twenty-three degrees below zero with the wind-chill and he was in danger of frostbite. The wind blew fiercely and whistled around the house making it impossible to hear his calls. In desperation, he jumped out of the barrel into a snowbank and climbed the wintery hill by foot. When he walked into the house, he was purple with cold and rage. He decided, right then and there, that the ski lift had to go and could not be dissuaded. I disagreed. As crazy as the system was, I did not think there was any alternative.

One weekend, I took Scott and Erin to visit Gloria, Ray, and their cousins in Lowville. While we were gone, Ron dismantled the entire lift, cable, and motor, and disposed of it all. I was shocked when we arrived home. The following few years of winters were difficult. Leaving the house or returning was such an undertaking that we hesitated to go anywhere. Years later, we bought a snowmobile and a sleigh attachment. This helped to a degree, although it was quite dangerous to go all the way up the steep snowy incline considering a sharp cliff ran along one side. Without constant vigilance during the ascension, the snowmobile could easily have gone over the cliff and flipped with us underneath it. In addition, the driver had to accelerate at a tremendous speed to reach the hilltop or it would conk out in the middle of the hill and skid or roll back down. To drive the rate of speed that was necessary to climb the hill was a recipe for catastrophe. It was exciting to ride on the flat open fields, but as a tool to reach the house, the snowmobile was not practical.

The property and home improvements seemed endless. Eventually, we added a lovely addition to the front of the house, which became a cozy living room, half-bath and a loft style library-like bedroom. We insulated those rooms, so they stayed warm. We also built a giant deck around two sides of the house with a live pine tree growing up through the middle. I used a mop and turpentine to strip the deck and then stained it with creosote. I really enjoyed the do-it-yourself approach of improving our first home as a family, although I wondered later whether those chemicals contributed to illnesses I suffered later in my life.

DEATH AND EDGAR CAYCE

Our East Berne neighbors generally watched out for each other and were kind. Although the homes were far apart, we tried to keep our eyes out for anything unusual. An elderly woman, Esther, lived down the street in a tiny three-room cottage. She contacted me one day to say her husband, Joe, was terribly ill. They could not convince our town's general practitioner, Dr. Smith whose office was only a mile away, to come to their home. The couple had no car and Joe was too sick to get out of his chair. I rushed over to see if I could help and found the poor man sitting stiff and upright in his chair. He had stopped breathing and Esther, who was deaf and legally blind, did not realize that her husband had died. When I called Dr. Smith, she said there was nothing she could do at this time, as she was busy with other patients. She did not see the need if Joe was already deceased, to make the drive to Esther's house. Following this callous incident, our family never returned to her practice. Rather, we traveled to Albany for any medical care, and, from my perspective, the trip was worth the effort, so we didn't have to see Dr. Smith again.

The Rocks, a large, bohemian family lived a few miles down the road. Marcia and Bob had seven children, Ricky, Robbie, Jeannie, Chrissy, Stephie, Mikey, and Missy. The Rocks quickly became our closest friends on the mountain and that was a wonderful thing for Scott and Erin who finally had many children with whom to play in this desolate countryside. Together, the children would have a grand time on the tire swing hanging from a massive oak tree in their front yard. Hide and seek was a great challenge and lots of fun as they would count backwards from ten, then seek for the hidden in the Rock's old farmhouse, which was always abuzz with free-range chickens clucking, many loving scruffy dogs, and cats galore. Bob taught Erin and I to play acoustic guitar. On warm summer afternoons, we would spend hours on the front porch strumming tunes by Bob Dylan, Crosby, Stills and Nash, and more. Time spent with The Rocks was nourishing for everyone.

One of the many special qualities about The Rocks was their strong belief in the Hereafter. Based on their readings of the late, well-known seer, Edgar Cayce, they believed that our bodies are an encasement and that our souls live on after death. The rationale was that we return many times after this life, and we pay our karmic debts each time we come back.

Initially, I admit that I was skeptical of our friends' seemingly wishful fantasies. I consider myself agnostic. I believe that no God would condone the terrible tragedies that I witnessed in my life: war, atrocities, hunger, and disease. The philosophy of reincarnation and karma piqued my interest, and I researched the ideology extensively. I had meaningful discussions with Marcia, Bob, Ron, and close friends and found insight in Edgar Cayce's reasoning and ideology. I felt a sense of clarification to some of life's concerns that I pondered. My thoughts centered on the experience of my deep and overwhelming love of my siblings and parents. I suffered every fall, cut, bruise, or illness for them. It was far beyond empathy. I could not relax as a child or adult as I was afraid of what might befall them. Worry consumed me most of the time. It felt like they were my children, not my parents, brothers, or sister. I reasoned that they existed in my past lives, always in a loving capacity. In this life, I felt responsible to love and care for them. Paying karmic debts for something done in a previous life resonated with me. It gave reason to return to the living world. Having discovered this revelation, I first heard from Marcia and Bob Rock, I gained a better understanding of my thoughts and emotions. I became a firm believer in the philosophy of reincarnation.

I will never forget the date, June 15, 1967. It was a deeply mournful day for me. I received a phone call that woke me and Ron in the middle of the summer night. A doctor from New York Presbyterian Hospital delivered the news that, at the age of 55, my beloved mother had succumbed to breast cancer. My grief was unbearable. I was despondent. High on our hill, we stood and watched out the window as a thunder and lightning storm raged in the night sky. I felt Mum leave this earth with a bang and Mum's passing brought to me a sorrow that eclipsed all others.

While my mother was dying in the hospital, Freda told us that they could not afford to make the trip from England so that Ivor could say his last goodbyes. She would not allow him to come alone as her jealousy remained sharp. My brother had not seen our mother in over 10 years due to his controlling wife and his inability to stand up to her. It was a tragedy.

Weeks later, the Rocks invited us to a grand picnic on their property. Given my state and still in deep mourning, I did not want to attend or socialize. I could not escape my grief, and nothing seemed to help me pass through it, but Ron insisted that I go to the picnic. He felt it could be healing for me to get out and see our dear friends. Reluctantly, I went along. The picnic was held in a beautiful clearing in the dense woods near the Rocks' home. I got out of the car and stood with uncertainty nearby. I did not want to speak with anyone for fear of bursting into tears. I needed some space before trying to mingle.

Within moments, a friend approached me and said, "I don't want to scare you, but my psychic friend watched you get out of your car. She said a beautiful lady was standing beside you. She was wearing a full-length turquoise gown and wore elegant, long, dangling earrings. Her hair was jet black and curled to perfection. Her lips were a brilliant wine color. She was close to you with her arm around your waist and was smiling."

The psychic asked her if I had lost someone close to me recently. I was in shock. My hand covered my mouth as I gasped. I felt faint. Only my family had known my mother, what she looked like, or that the last function we had attended together was my brother Brian's wedding. My mother had worn a long turquoise gown. Her hair was jet black and always styled with those perfect curls. Long, dangling earrings were her signature. The psychic told me that I should put my mind at rest. My mother was beside me to comfort me and see me through this sorrowful time. My past doubts of the Hereafter were dispelled at that moment, and I knew Mum was with me.

My sister-in-law, Yvonne, had kindly taken over the funeral arrangements and told me that my mother was buried in that turquoise dress. The Jewish faith doesn't have open viewings at their funerals, so I was unaware of this until she revealed this to me years later.

The Rocks were nomads at heart. They bought a large old school bus and turned it into a home for all nine of them along with a few dogs and cats. They decided to homeschool their children and travel the countryside until they landed in the next place where they would call home. They were a brief gift to us and touched our lives tremendously. I expect to meet them once again, if not in this life, in the next.

Within a week after the incident at the picnic at the Rocks, a clock on my wall that was previously in Mum's apartment, started to run backwards. I could not correct the problem. Our friend's husband was an electrician and always fixed one thing or another. I asked him if he could fix my clock. He told me that this sort of clock had one motor movement that could only go in one direction. It could not possibly go backward. He kept it at his house for a week or two and it ran perfectly for him, but not for me upon its return to me. Soon after, the alarm clock started to ring at odd times of the day. We never set it as an alarm, just used it as a clock in the living room. Many months later after my father moved nearby, I told him what the clocks did and how the alarm drove us crazy. He took them to his trailer and let them run for a few days. The alarm never went off unless he tested it to go off at a particular time. Otherwise, it ran smoothly and on time while he had them. In both cases, when I took them home, they continued to react the same way in my house as they had before.

When speaking later with Marcia and Bob about my clock experience, they were compelled to tell me that, when a person in the other life wanted to get the attention of a living loved one, the connection would most often be made during the daytime with a familiar object. Because I often looked at that clock both for practical and sentimental reasons, Mum had chosen to use that clock as a vehicle to communicate with me, to let me know she was thinking about me, and that she loved me. After hearing this, once again, I felt bathed in love. I knew Mum had not yet left my side and was with me, Ron, Scott, and Erin.

This feeling continued for several years, until I felt that she was finally able to move forward to gain knowledge, and to see other spirits that had crossed over years before. I believe she knew I was ready to let go.

DAD

After many years of estrangement, my father arrived from Elgin, Illinois, to live on our property at the bottom of our hill. He bought a nice mobile home. He purchased a navy blue Volkswagen Bug for his newly constructed garage. He was very pleased with his new abode and it was wonderful to have him so close after so many years apart. We enjoyed family gatherings, and the children had a granddad to enrich their lives. I believe my mother's death was the gateway for my dad's sudden appearance.

Dad had a special relationship with young Erin. He lovingly taught her all about wildflowers, bird species, classical music, and fine art. She learned from him how to recognize different plants and to plant seeds and bulbs. He gave her various projects to paint or sew and had her help him with building functional sculptures. She could easily identify many classical composers and fine artists. She learned how to draw exceptionally well. She was reading complete books at three-years-old because of Dad's patient instruction. She was an intelligent child and Dad spent the time nurturing her intellectual growth.

Conversely, Dad had little tolerance for Scott, who was nine years old when Dad joined us. Scott felt the huge loss of his admiring grandmother and would have clung to any endearments from my father, but Dad gave none. Scott could do no wrong in my mother's eyes, whereas my father could find in him no right. My heart broke for my young son. Dad paid him no attention. It reminded me of being a child and watching him ignore or behave cruelly toward my siblings while behaving marvelously toward me. It was difficult for me to tolerate Dad's behavior, but Ron was enraged.

I gave Dad the popular psychology book, I'm OK, You're OK, in hopes that he, as the adult, could recognize the blame and criticism he generated and what that was doing to his grandson's young mind. Unfortunately, nothing worked. I was deeply saddened. Meanwhile, Erin blossomed with her granddad around.

KELLY GIRL

I found part-time work as a Kelly Girl and I was assigned to various companies to fill temporary vacancies for regular employees who had maternity or disability leaves of absence. Primarily, I worked as a secretary for doctors, lawyers, and writers. I never knew the terms of each assignment, but I knew I did not have to stay at it forever and that was the perfect situation for me. Also, I could leave Erin with Dad when she got home from kindergarten. At eleven-years-old, Scott was able to take care of himself well enough until I got home.

On one of my trips to an Albany office, I drove our Volkswagen Bus through Thacher Park. On a summer day, the views were spectacular and overlooked waterfalls and a dramatic 1,200-foot escarpment. However, if you were driving through the park in the winter, the roads were often treacherous. There was a vertical rock face to my right and on my left side was another 1,200-foot drop to the bottom of the park. Snow and ice had fallen the night before, so the road was dangerous and slippery. The car abruptly took a spin that seemed never ending.

I did not use the brakes as that could have been even more hazardous. Instead, as speed gathered, I got down on the floor and waited for the end to come. No cars approached from the other lane and there was nothing to stop me if I hurtled to crash into one cliffside or tumble over the other. I waited for what seemed a lifetime for the whirling to end. Eventually, the spinning ceased, and the car sat dead still in the middle of the downward trend. I slowly got up off the floor to see where I was. To my utter amazement, the car had stopped all by itself on the thick ice. I crawled back into my driver's seat and sat silent and shaking from head to toe. I asked repeatedly, "How did I survive this? Why did I survive this?"

At another one of my placements, I was employed in a doctor's office. On the first day we experienced a torrential rainstorm. The office was on the basement level where a dozen tall file cabinets were stored. Suddenly, we heard rushing water as it poured down the stairs to our level. The other women and I grabbed our coats and handbags and sloshed out of the room as water cascaded into the office. As we all got out the door, the file cabinets fell and floated around the room. They knocked the office door shut and we hoped we had rescued all our personal belongings as there was no way to get back in.

My little yellow Volkswagen Bug that we had recently bought stayed afloat in the parking lot in about three feet of water. Advertisements for the Bug had shown that it floated and was still drivable. I got in and decided to drive the twenty-three miles home right through the water-filled streets of Albany. The police were out in force in the city and they stood knee deep in water. There was no traffic anywhere. Me and my little Bug were the only idiots on the road. The police just looked on in awe and never tried to stop me. As advertised, my car floated and handled well as I steered my way out of town. Once I reached the cliffs that led up to Thacher Park, the water flowed downhill and away from the road. I merely drove through low puddles the rest of the way home.

I took another Kelly Girl part-time job working for the State University of New York at Albany (SUNY Albany). I worked in their Humanistic Education Department, which was housed on private grounds that had been donated to the university. It was originally owned by Mayor Erastus Corning. The stone cottage where I worked had been a charming life-sized playhouse for Mayor Corning's daughter. The office was very cozy, and I enjoyed both the work and atmosphere. It felt like I worked with one big happy family. When asked if I would like to stay on full-time, I gladly responded yes. This job was a dream come true.

Working in the Humanistic Education Department at SUNY Albany was a terrific learning experience for me. I had never been to college, and I gleaned all I could from the documents I typed each day. The 11 professors for whom I worked were absolutely wonderful and they generously shared their knowledge. When I asked about some of the interesting concepts that I had typed for them, they invited me to take a few moments and join them on the couches by the fireplace while they discussed their ideas.

The department ran week-long seminars for teachers and professors from various colleges in New York State. I was fortunate to be able to attend these sessions. The main house, which had eight bedrooms, lodged the visiting teachers and administrative professionals who attended the courses. The facility had a cook and full-time staff who took care of the house. When there were no teachers in residence, staff was permitted to enjoy the gourmet cuisine and each other's company. On holidays, we celebrated together and brought our families along for grand parties in the mansion.

I had begun to practice Hatha Yoga and, in inclement weather, used the house to do my exercises during lunch. The professors and staff were intrigued and wanted to learn, so I taught them. One of the stances was called the lion pose in which we got down on all fours, stretched our heads towards the ceiling and stuck out our tongues. There was plenty of laughter and we all enjoyed the camaraderie. It felt good to give back my knowledge in exchange for theirs.

During the time I worked at SUNY Albany, the terrible war raged in Vietnam. Ron and I disagreed with the policies of President Nixon when he wanted to place mines in the harbor at Haiphong. In my opinion, it was a plan with potentially catastrophic results. We believed President Nixon's decision would affect the Red Cross ships that traversed the oceans and administered medical help to so many in need. These ships would need to sail through that mine-infested harbor.

By this time, Ron was a public relations director for Governor Hugh Carey and had many pearls of wisdom about ways we could stage a protest. We sent letters and telegrams to senators and representatives in Washington D.C. to protest the mines in Haiphong Harbor. Early on, we didn't know the official position SUNY Albany would take on the issue and neither of us wanted to lose our jobs for being agitators, especially given our past experiences. We went home and did things our own way instead of with a group.

Encouragingly, however, there were protests across the nation and many universities were united in their criticism of President Nixon's plan. Our section of the university closed and stopped work until Nixon's decision was lifted. Unfortunately, we accomplished little. In the end, the Haiphong Harbor Ship Channel was lined with mines.

In 1972, I asked for vacation time to visit England. I dreamt that I lost my Aunt Jenny, Mum's sister, and felt the need to see her and my other relatives. I was traveling alone as the fares were far above what we could afford for our family of four.

During the time I was gone, the government made cuts to the budget for arts and humanities. The department in which I worked was shut down. They did not let me know while I was away as my employer thought it would spoil my holiday. Had I known; I would have stayed longer than the three weeks I requested. I had not been home in twelve years, and there was still so much to catch up on and many more hugs to give.

When I returned to New York, I discovered the news about the dissolution of my job and the whole department. I met with some of the people with whom I had worked, and we shed some tears. We had worked together in such a lovely atmosphere during the years we spent there. We had created our own utopia with kind and caring people around us daily. I knew it would be difficult to recreate such a nurturing work environment again.

RESET

After my return from England, I suffered from stomach ailments with violent diarrhea and vomiting. My misery and pain were constant. My condition worsened and, eventually, was hospitalized. They discovered I had a spastic colon and hiatal hernia, and I was prescribed medication and a diet to alleviate these problems.

Life became easier once I felt healthier. Ron and I decided to take Scott and Erin to the beautiful Island of Bermuda on holiday. It was a magical time for all of us. We snorkeled by day and took wonderful dinner cruises into the aqua blue sea each evening. We built sandcastles and relaxed on the pink sandy beaches of Horseshoe Bay. Erin got her first sunburn. So did I.

Ron and the children were out in the bay swimming having a grand time, so I went in for a dip myself. I was not a swimmer and was in fact afraid of the sea. It looked so beautiful, and I was getting very warm in the sun, so I decided to brave the waves. I barely took one step into the ocean when a massive wave came along, picked me up, and dragged me out to sea. The rip tide was far too strong for me to fight, and the waves repeatedly rolled me over and under. My head remained under water so I could not shout for help. I believed this was the end. I could do nothing but hold my breath and let the waves take me on my journey. My unexpected attitude of acceptance and calm prevented me from panicking, and I held my breath without strain. Before long, although it felt like eternity, I was slapped back onto the warm pink beach. I lay down gently on my towel. My family never knew of my terrifying experience. I have never been swimming in the sea again.

During our trip, Scott was intrigued by the intricate workings of the hotel, bar and restaurants. The seed was planted, and he knew he wanted to work in that industry. After Scott graduated high school, he attended Paul Smith's College and studied Hotel and Restaurant Management and continues to work in that industry to this day.

Soon after our holiday in Bermuda, I had surgery on both hips to remove non-cancerous lipomas. It took some time to heal. For weeks, I lay face down on the couch as lying on my back was too painful. It was difficult to read or watch TV while in that position, so I had a lot of time to think. During this time of forced reflection, I realized that I wanted to volunteer and help people in my area to thrive. I found a group that was the perfect fit.

After my recovery, I volunteered for a charitable group called Fish. The name evolved from the symbol of early Christians as a sign of unity and identity. Fish assisted with clothing, transportation, medicine, food, and shelter. We called around to create a network of willing volunteers to assist the less fortunate, elderly, and disabled. We found and provided rides to people without vehicles so they could get to doctors, grocery stores, and pharmacies.

In 1974, the cost of gas suddenly skyrocketed. Gas was in short supply, and few could afford it even when it was available. This was a major obstacle for Fish as rides slowly ceased to exist. Our volunteers could not afford the gas needed to provide the charitable rides. Many underprivileged people we assisted needed to find alternate ways of transportation. Many could no longer get to their needed services. The situation concerned me a great deal and I hatched an idea. Instead of individual rides, I thought Fish could provide a bus and give the same services to many more individuals collectively.

We lived in a rural area with homes miles apart from one another. The logistics required to run a bus around the countryside seemed impossible. At first, I thought maybe we could have a bus that stopped at specific locations, like the post office, general store, and library. However, getting people to those points of pickup was just as awkward as getting them to Albany, 20 miles away. I decided to try and set up a bus that went to the home of each person in need of a ride to Albany.

The next challenge was the huge job of making calls to many institutions that I thought might consider charitable contributions. I desperately needed to raise funds to get this bus idea off the ground. Most of the organizations I contacted about donations thought it was a good idea, but funds simply were not available. I finally got help from one company that worked only in the inner-city of Albany for the poor. They agreed to send a bus and a driver to the "hill towns" of Berne, East Berne and Westerlo. After dozens of calls to the Fish members, I established a network of people who gave their phone numbers to anyone who needed to get to a doctor or other important appointments in the Albany area. We collectively gathered information and my team let me know who wanted to use the bus and where they needed to go. I made intricate charts, so no one was left behind. People who never had the convenience of their own transportation were suddenly able to get out and do their necessary things. I was also able to extend the trips to include one shopping center each week.

Additionally, a clinic in Albany was offered as a healthcare resource to our group. Early on, some of the young people needed vaccinations, but they were fearful. The only way I could demonstrate that it was not a big deal was for me to have a flu shot performed in front of them so they could see I would not faint or drop dead. Doing so, I built trust to the point which the reluctant felt comfortable receiving the vaccination they needed. Our patrons were so pleased to live through the procedure.

Unfortunately, all good things come to an end. Funds for that organization eventually did run dry. I could not bear to let those people lose what they had cherished, this sense of freedom. I called other agencies. I spoke to the Department of Transportation and the Public Transit Corporation, and they turned me down outright. They said the cost for each person to go one way from Berne to Albany would be five dollars, which was too expensive.

A newspaper called and asked me what our next plan was to provide transportation. I told them about the numerous roadblocks I faced, including the Public Transit Corporation. I explained that they would not come to the countryside because of the cost and would not provide the services. The story appeared in the newspaper and the following day my phone rang. The Public Transit Corporation felt remorse about the situation after seeing the article and they offered a Mercedes bus that held twenty passengers. I gave them the route information we had gathered, and the service was offered at no charge to the riders.

Many people called me during that time and thanked me because I helped them get out from between their four walls. Patrons expressed that they had not been able to get to their various services until the bus came into existence. On a trip back to Berne 27-years later, I learned that the bus service still ran at least one day a week. I was elated and felt a great sense of accomplishment.

BEYOND BUSES

During the time I was coordinating transportation for those in need, I also became aware of many residents who were living under other dire circumstances. The phone calls we began to receive veered away from requests for the use of the bus and more toward those whose needs were more profound.

Certified social workers helped many of these people, but the red tape and paperwork that the social workers encountered didn't allow them to do much in a timely manner. I privately aided some people and often went beyond what a social worker could do. Sometimes, people just needed to talk about their problems and sort out various solutions without all the pressure of interviews and forms. Many often felt like a number in the system. People were scared and often felt judged. Typical callers were young mothers who could not feed their children. Others included abused women, elderly individuals, and people with severe illnesses. They needed various services but did not know where to begin.

Ron pleaded with me not to visit the homes of the people I helped. He felt, rightly so, that any family member could be potentially violent. Some people do not take kindly to charity. He did not want me to be on the wrong side of such a situation.

One couple lived as caretakers in a tiny shack at a junkyard where cars were demolished. The couple had enough room next to the dump for a small corral where they kept a pony for their adopted daughter who had severe brain damage. The woman herself was barely able to care for her family, much less a pony. She was diabetic and had some of her toes amputated. She was sick often and had trouble monitoring her condition. I searched local charity organizations and obtained a wheelchair, bedpan, cane, and various other items she desperately needed. I brought all the items to her. On this visit I brought Erin with me. I knew Ron would not be pleased, but I did so anyway. The couple wasn't comfortable receiving charity and wanted to give something in return for my efforts. They gave me a full bale of hay from the pony's corral. Although I had absolutely no use for it, I thanked them profusely. My little yellow Volkswagen Bug had a trunk in the front of the car instead of the back. The hay stuck out of the trunk on all sides, and my car looked like it had a mouthful of food. When I drove up my driveway Scott and my Dad had a good laugh. Thankfully, Ron wasn't home from work yet, so he was unaware that Erin had come along.

Another family I helped was in the town I lived in, East Berne. The parents, Rudy and Arlene, and their four children lived in a house in which few of the windows had glass and many were boarded over. I went to their home without Ron's knowledge. Again, I took young Erin with me. There was a broken toilet, a rusty spigot with water that dripped into an ancient kitchen sink, and a general aroma of decay and mildew. Their house had dirt floors, a potbelly stove in one room, and little insulation to keep in what little heat it generated. The family sat around the stove all winter in coats, hats, and gloves because it was so terribly cold inside. I worried about the bare insulation in one of the children's bedrooms because of her asthma, so I nailed up a bunch of my old sheets to help cover the draft. We came home covered in welts from flea bites and didn't tell Ron how we had come by them. I found an agency to provide insulation and we would install it ourselves. The children and I managed to get the insulation installed, although it was nowhere near a professional job. In retrospect, it was dangerous for my daughter and I to go into their home as the husband, Rudy, was known for having quite a foul temper.

Trouble brewed when I arranged for the children to attend a Red Cross camp for a week in the summer to holiday away from their poverty. The children were overjoyed when the Red Cross bus picked them up. When Rudy came home from work and found out where his children were, he went berserk. He got in his truck, drove to the camp, and dragged his four children home. He literally burned the new clothes the Red Cross had given each of them. He said, "My kids don't need charity from anyone," ending the only vacation those children had ever had in their young lives. This broke my heart.

When Arlene wanted to get a job to help buy clothes for the children, her husband forbade it. He was a proud and stubborn man with a scary mean streak. Quietly, she made other plans. Arlene wanted to leave Rudy because of his unreasonable and sometimes violent behavior. She needed an education and a diploma to get a decent job. A group of Fish volunteers, a social worker, and I collectively drove her to classes each week until she earned her diploma. I do not believe Rudy ever found out. After her youngest child was born, Rudy did not bother to visit her or the baby in the hospital. She went home, healed, and filed for divorce. Life became so much better for her and her children once the divorce was granted and she moved out of the house. She secured a good job working for the courts and found a safe and warm home, and eventually a lovely new husband.

With help from Dad, I started a youth center in our town. I wanted to provide a safe place for young people who had no other place to go during weekends and school breaks to enjoy fun activities. We received the donation of a decent size vacant building on a main roadway with an adjacent parking lot. Dad, Scott, and I made what had been a broken-down mess into a pleasant and usable safe haven for the community youth. For weeks, we painted walls, repaired broken plumbing, scrubbed old pots and pans, and improved the kitchen by adding a pass-through counter into a great room. Scott painted a beautiful outdoor sign for the youth center. All volunteers were greeted warmly considering we needed a lot of manpower. Someone graciously donated an abundance of folding chairs. We white-washed a large wall to serve as the screen to project rented movies.

I ordered the first movie to debut at our theater from our local library. I requested something suitable for young children and teenagers. There was great excitement at the youth center on our movie night launch and we had a full house. Dad started up the projector and the screen filled with the title of what we were about to see. I cannot recall what the title was, but it was a movie that clearly stated in large letters, "For adults only." The first scene showed explicit sex. Thankfully, the blue movie aired for only a flash. Dad was quick on the draw and shut down the whole thing in a flash. I nearly fainted when I saw the reaction of kids and parents alike. I never ordered another movie again. We designated that important task to someone else.

Ron in the United States Airforce, 1953.

Elaine and Ron's engagement photograph in
Chiswick, London, 1953.

Ron and Elaine at Rosalee and Al's new
post-war home, Lee Close, Walthamstow,
East London, 1953.

Elaine in the chicken coop, Gladstone, Missouri,
1955.

Elaine pregnant with Scott in Chiswick, London, 1959.

Elaine, Queen for the day, 1961.

The Rock family, 1972.

Gloria and Ray at their trailor in
Norwich, NY, 1960.

Scott, 6 years old, Erin 6 months old in
Norwich, NY, 1965.

Our home in East Berne, NY, 1974.

Brian, Gloria, Dad, Elaine, Ivor family reunion, East
Berne, NY, 1975.

Newspaper article about our ski lift in East Berne, NY, 1967.

PART III

DIVORCE

While I focused on doing my thing and was involved in other people's lives between the youth center and the area bus, Ron expressed that he felt useless to me. Nothing was further from the truth as I felt I could not have done any of it without his support.

Around that time, Ron and I made friends with a couple, Carol and Dennis, who lived locally. They were younger intellectuals, and both were artists. Unfortunately, their marriage was dissolving, and Carol was devastated by this. She confided this to Ron and leaned on him, which helped Ron feel useful again. Carol seemed to need him more than I did, or so Ron thought. Ron was in the right place at the right time and a romance sprouted.

Soon Ron declared he had fallen in love with Carol and was leaving me. Once again, I felt like I had been knocked down and would never recover. My familiar depression reared its head once more. I was not eating properly and was rail thin. Within weeks, I was diagnosed with mononucleosis and was confined to bed for six weeks. Depression added to the problem and intensified my thoughts of what this might mean to the children and to me. Scott was about to graduate from high school and move away for college. Erin was the tender age of 12 with many changes about to slam into her young body and mind.

I had already experienced this misery with Ron in England when Scott was a baby. I would see history repeated. I knew I had to leave, get on with my life, and let him get on with his. I told him that if I stayed, I would be concerned each time we were angry at each other and I would worry if he were gone longer than usual from the house, that he would be with Carol. The trust was broken.

We had our house listed for sale and I went looking for an apartment in Clifton Park. The town in Saratoga County had an excellent school district, which was obviously important for Erin. Ron and I could live close to each other and co-parent more easily. Weeks before we sold the house and moved out, Ron decided that he didn't want to go through with it and asked, "Can we forget the whole thing and stay together?"

Although in many ways it seemed almost impossible to do, I felt that I might have a chance to start anew. I was 42-years-old and, I hoped, had many years to potentially rebuild my life. I loved Ron and life without him seemed unimaginable, but I believed that I had to be strong in my resolve. Not only was I totally heartbroken, but the situation was also terrible for Scott and Erin.

I managed to move forward with my life as a single mother. It was painful and often difficult. However, I knew I could find the strength I had cultivated so many years ago as that young girl in Somerset, witnessing bombs dropped on London, touching the sad faces of war criminals to brighten their day, and surviving many nights without my dear family.

I found a condominium in Clifton Park for Erin and I to live in. Previously, Erin had attended a small country school with a total of 400 students. Her new school in the Shenendehowa School District was vastly larger with around 10,000 students, a big change for Erin, but it offered many exciting classes for her along with an excellent staff.

Scott went off to Paul Smith's College near Lake Placid and studied hospitality management as he had dreamed after our family trip to Bermuda. Like his Mum and sister, Scott faced many changes in his life, but Scott had seemingly been adaptive to this new situation, as he was during our flight over the Atlantic Ocean on the troop plane when we first traveled to the United States all those years ago.

Ron moved to a condo near Erin and me so he could spend time with his daughter. Erin needed her dad as much as she needed me. The experience was traumatic for her to leave the home and friends she had known essentially all her life. The change would prove to be difficult for all of us.

SINGLE MOM

Life as a single mother was devastatingly difficult and amazingly liberating at the same time. I wanted to date, but it was all so strange to me. I could not imagine having a conversation with another man, let alone anything more intimate. I was not confident and rather intimidated by the thought of it all.

One evening after Erin went to bed, the father of her friend Christine, knocked on my door. He was a huge man with thick gray hair, a deep tan, and a slight accent. We had never formally met, but I saw him around the complex and knew who he was. I invited him in, as I thought he wanted to talk about our girls.

We chatted for a short while and he suddenly put his arms around me and forcefully kissed me. In an instant, his hands seemed to be everywhere on my body, but I had done nothing to lead him on. He became stronger and more powerful by the minute, and I struggled to get him away from me. I wanted to scream, but my immediate thought was not to disturb Erin in case she came into the living room. I repeatedly hit him and pushed him away and didn't make much sound but for thumps and bumps while I scratched and bit him. He finally got the message, thank heaven, because I was thoroughly exhausted and did not know how long I could hold out.

After he left, I was in complete shock. I had not disturbed Erin, which was important to me. Days later I discovered more about him from a neighbor. His ex-wife was a writer who had published a book about his life as a Greek gangster and his involvement with organized crime. She had spitefully written secrets about his life, and he was not safe after the book was published. Shortly after he accosted me, his car was set on fire in our parking lot by his warring rivals. Under these circumstances, I feared for our safety, so Erin and I moved from this otherwise beautiful complex. We stayed in Clifton Park and rented a small cottage.

I worked for the New York State Bar Association on a special assignment at the New York State Education Department. It was impossible to concentrate on work. I felt alone and depressed because of Ron's infidelity and our divorce. I would often cry as I typed and could not read the words through the blur of my tears.

One day when I went to the loo to pull myself together, a woman who was about my age was apparently there for the same reason. She was visibly upset and I asked her if she was all right. She told me her name was Jean and that she was in the process of divorcing her husband and also had a teenage girl. Jean and I commiserated, talked about our worry for our daughters who were home alone while each of us worked. With so much in common, we became good friends.

Jean and I discussed methods of self-care as we faced the challenges of living as single mothers. With Jean's support and a new sense of resolve, I took a course at the local high school and learned to tune-up my car, which included how to change the tires, the functions of the distributor cap and spark plugs, and how to change oil and filters. I taught Erin what I had learned. Even though I knew little, I could sound knowledgeable enough to talk basics with the mechanics and could stop them when they tried to fix unnecessary things or take advantage of me. It was good for me to have that feeling of independence and confidence.

My former supervisor at the New York State Bar Association, Al Petrillo, called me to say that he was in the midst of a divorce. He had heard I was in a bad state of mind since my split with Ron and asked if I would like to go to dinner with him.

Fourteen years my junior, Al had been a good boss and he and I had always communicated well. Al was also charming and handsome, and I felt a sense of safety confiding in him. Al became a good friend and, eventually, a lover.

We cared a great deal for each other as we shared our joys and our sadness. While our relationship intensified, however, I made a firm decision as a single mother to a teenage daughter, not to move in with a man and live under the same roof.

By the summer of 1978, Al and I decided to make a trip to England and take Erin with us. We gathered our passports and luggage and set off for London. Upon our arrival, my family made Al feel welcome, while Erin enjoyed the company of her cousins, aunts, and uncles. I was eager to visit my brother, Ivor. I arrived at his home to surprise him and his wife, Freda. Ivor answered the front door and nearly fell over from shock. He was thrilled and hugged and kissed us and whirled me around in his joy. I could hear Freda yell out from the back of the house, "Who is it?" Ivor shouted, "Can you believe it? It's Elaine all the way from America!" Freda replied, "Tell her to come back another time, I'm watching television." Ivor sheepishly told us we must go as Freda was otherwise engaged. My heart sank as I left him. Freda ruled the roost with an iron fist. There was no reasoning with her, and by this point in their marriage, Ivor never attempted to question her motives. He always obeyed.

Although I was very heartbroken, we toured the city of London and then traveled to the Dorset countryside where we stayed with my lifelong friend, Pam Gentle whose family took me in during the war as an evacuee. It was lovely to reconnect now during better times. We laughed and cried as Pam, and I talked, and I remembered with fondness the kindness her family had shown me all those years ago. Sadly, Pam's parents had passed, so I was not able to express to them my genuine feelings of love I had for them.

The three of us continued to Somerset and stayed with Pam's sister, Beryl, who was ensconced in a difficult marriage herself. I believe seeing Al and I happily together urged her to get the divorce she had mulled over in her mind for years. Seeing these places with fresh eyes and years from the war was healing for me. Building new memories with my daughter in these places from my past meant the world to me.

The feelings I had for Al were, apparently, not completely reciprocated. Upon our return to Albany, Al began a relationship with his secretary. Considering my experience with Ron, I had learned the lesson that I would not tolerate infidelity, although Al and I did remain platonic friends.

Al eventually married his secretary. Later, after his wife had a hysterectomy, Al called and asked me to have dinner with him. I knew that he had more than dinner on his mind. My response was a resolute, "No, thank you."

My heart was still tender, and I struggled to brace my nerves as I once again considered dating. I was not savvy and felt awkward when it came to dealing with men as a single woman. I found a group for singles and asked Jean to join me as we both felt self- conscious going alone. To my surprise, it was a great group with many activities including dancing, tennis, skiing, camping, book reviews, wine and cheese parties, and white-water canoeing. The group also had discussions where members talked about the benefits and disadvantages of being single, dating, parenting, and finding love.

At times, neither Jean nor I wanted to go out, but we urged each other so that we would not become stagnant. Going out and dating made our days and evenings less lonely. We enjoyed many laughs about our singles group experiences. Even if we didn't enjoy some of the dates we had, we enjoyed each other and built a lifelong friendship.

I took a full-time job in the New York State Assembly as a secretary to an assemblyman's assistant. The assistant was totally incompetent and barely capable of stringing the words together for a single memo. She wrote and rewrote continually; a six-line invitation or note for the assemblyman would take a whole day. When I could no longer stand it, I had a long chat with her about her lack of professionalism. I taught her secretarial skills including filing, wording letters to politicians, writing to constituents, and methods not to waste taxpayers' time and money. I was astounded when she said that she respected me more after being so upfront with her about her office practices. She was young and naive, and I was glad she listened to me.

Months later, she called me to ask if I would like to join her and her husband at their home for dinner. Her father-in-law would be there, and she wanted us to meet. Her father-in-law was a kind gentleman and the four of us had a great evening together. Afterward, we even went on a few dates together.

My position as the assistant's secretary was not as pleasant. I had been the 13th person who had worked for the young assistant in less than a year. Even after the patient training I offered, I could not tolerate her ignorance and searched for another job during my lunch hours.

I interviewed for a position with Marty Solomon, the New York State senator from Brooklyn. He was not a sociable person, had a dry personality, and lacked a sense of humor. Nonetheless, I took the job that he offered and never once regretted my decision. I began as his assistant. He was the only one working in his office and had a slim budget. I quickly became his executive secretary, and my responsibilities grew. I interviewed and hired an attorney for his Albany office. Each year thereafter, I hired at least four or five college interns who worked for credit toward bachelor's degrees.

Before I started working for Marty, I did not understand the intricate structure of the government, but the job gave me the opportunity to get a free education while getting paid. The work was fascinating. I met many people who came to Albany to lobby for interests and rights. I answered correspondence from constituents, which the senator read and signed if he approved. I researched bills and went to the senate floor to watch debates. I was privileged to hear opposing sides and try to understand these different viewpoints. I provided Marty the information I had learned to update him about each bill. The more research my job required, the more knowledge I acquired for my own education.

This sort of public service nourished me, particularly when I was able to directly help people. My salary was almost a bonus considering I was being paid to do the work that I loved. One day, we received an interesting letter at the office. A family wrote to say that their 82-year-old father had fought in World War II, had been wounded, and had earned a Purple Heart, but never received his medal. I proceeded to jump through bureaucratic hoops in Washington D.C. and the State Senate in Albany. The medal that he had earned so many years earlier was finally awarded to the elderly man. He and his family were delighted and proud. I felt a great sense of accomplishment to have been a part of this veteran's ceremony.

DIVORCED AND DATING

Needing to make the ends meet, I had to work more than one job. After a full day at the capital, I worked in the evenings as a coat-check person at The Cranberry Bog restaurant in Albany. I earned tip money which helped me scrape by. While working at the Cranberry Bog, I met a young, attractive waiter named Andy. He was also a ski instructor in Killington and a water ski instructor in Albany. Andy had dabbled in Hollywood in the porn industry. Ten-years my junior, Andy had quite a beautiful body and we got along famously.

During that summer, Andy taught me how to water-ski. That was a miracle if ever there was one. I did not care for having water in my face and could barely dog paddle. Yet, there I was on the Mohawk River water skiing behind a boat that belonged to his friend. It was amazing that I stayed up on the water for minutes, which felt like hours. I certainly partook in this solely for Andy's attention because I never water-skied after that.

Though I was never the outdoor type and had no great love for cold winter weather, Andy taught me how to downhill ski that winter. Andy and I took Erin and her friend, Amy, with us. Erin and Amy were members of the Shenendehowa High School ski club, so Erin was a proficient skier. Meanwhile, I was terrified.

On my very first run down the mountain at Killington, I fell and severely injured my knee. Andy wanted the stretchers brought to the mountain top so that I could be safely brought down to the first aid hut. I was too embarrassed. I insisted that I ski down the hill myself, which I did with great difficulty. That evening, Andy introduced me to marijuana, which took the edge off the pain of my injury and, the next morning, to drive back to Clifton Park.

After returning home, I discovered that I had torn the cartilage in my knee, which set me back a bit. I needed crutches for nearly five months during which time the romance with Andy ended. Andy was a fun person, and I enjoyed his vitality and his company. For me, that was all it was. We parted quite amicably.

In the meantime, I was unable to drive as I convalesced. Ron worked at the capitol in Albany as well, so he kindly drove me to and from work at the Senate during those five months until my ski injury healed. Would only that a heart could heal as quickly.

A brief relationship with a rabbi taught me that not all men of the cloth were to be trusted. I had zero romantic interest in this man, but I appreciated his amazing intelligence and knowledge of the Jewish faith. On our first date, he took me to dinner and quickly professed his love for me. When I expressed to him that I did not feel the same way, he immediately began to recite his own obituary as though he had just died. I was dumbfounded.

The next day, the rabbi came by my house to take me out again. As it happened, my Volkswagen Rabbit had been stolen from my driveway overnight. When the police called to say they found my car in a field, they warned me that the interior was damaged and was littered with beer cans and liquor bottles. A thick mud covered the exterior. Other than a few dents and scratches, the car seemed to be mechanically sound. What upset me the most was the fact that all my treasured car tools were stolen.

The rabbi joined me to pick up my car and advised that I should get the car washed before going to my insurance company for an estimate of the damage. I drove into the manual car wash, which had a hand-held hose and a circular, spiral hose of water jets that washed the undercarriage. Chivalrously, the rabbi placed quarters in the slot and took hold of the hand hose while I remained in the car. As he started to wash the car, the spiral water jets underneath the car began to spray and swirl. The spinning water jets were made for larger cars that were wider than my little Rabbit, so water sprayed everywhere and drenched the Rabbit, and the rabbi. He tried to look dignified and pretended nothing was out of the ordinary while he continued to wash the car . . . and himself. Afterward, we decided to have Chinese take-out and he asked me to go inside with him to order something for Erin. Water dripped down his face and from his clothes. He looked so ridiculous that I was mortified to be seen with him.

As strange as the car wash incident had been, the rabbi would further distinguish himself. I received a $400 income tax fund which was all I had to pay the rent. The rabbi promised that if I invested the money in trees for Israel, I would triple it in six weeks. He took my cash and I never saw it or him again. Months later, I told Senator Soloman about the money the rabbi had taken. He contacted the police and discovered the rabbi had pulled this stunt on many other unsuspecting women. He was married and had only a post office box for an address. By this point, I could not even believe this man was a rabbi. I never learned more about this strange and unscrupulous man. I was later told, however, that New York Police officers waited for him at his Brooklyn post office box when he picked up his mail and was arrested.

Uri was a history professor at SUNY-Albany who had lost his wife to cancer and was not yet at peace. He was still in the depths of his grief. I loved history and had read many books on the subject. It was that thread that attracted me to Uri and sparked my interest in him. I was the first woman Uri dated after he lost his wife. Curiously, Uri did not seem to know when to stop quoting historical references. No matter our conversation, he would unwaveringly take an historical tangent. Once when we were dancing while out on a date, he continued a history lesson throughout the waltz, the hustle, and the twist.

One fall day, Uri took me to a lovely lake in Massachusetts. He brought along his canoe, and we lazily paddled around on the water on a perfect autumn day. The color of the leaves that surrounded the lake as well as the stillness was beautiful. Surprisingly, Uri provided a history lesson that lasted the length of the trip. I noticed campsites in the distance. I wanted to row to the shore and see if there was a suitable place to camp with Erin in the future. He kindly paddled over and suggested I go explore the camp. He was not quite to the edge of the shoreline when I stood up and put one foot out on the sandy beach. Unfortunately, the other foot did not follow. One foot was on land and the other was still in the boat as he was trying to come to a stop. I did a split, and then fell into the lake. As I rose from the water, I laughed so hard that I could hardly speak. Uri did not see the humor in the situation. His concern was kind, but his worry and comments just went on and on all the way back across the lake, to the car, and during the entire trip back to Albany.

Uri was a good man and, in many ways, the most intelligent and sensitive man I had met. However, his awkwardness in conversation, his deep and unresolved grief, and his lack of an ability to recognize humor in life's laughable moments were more than enough to show me that we were not ultimately compatible.

I dated another smashing man who, like Uri, lost his wife to a battle with cancer. Bill was quite a bit older than me and so kind. He and I worked together and soon began dating. Bill had a sweet son, Michael, in his mid-20's. He had Down Syndrome and lived nearby his father in a group home. I found this lovely young man especially interesting. Bill interacted with his son beautifully and his love for Michael deeply touched me.

Bill, Michael, and I attended synagogue together. I visited them at Bill's home on several occasions. Michael would often ask me if I planned to marry his father. He said his dad really wanted me to. I felt sorrow for Bill and his son, however no romantic feelings developed for me towards Bill. I sensed that I was unable to take the place of someone so revered as his departed wife.

Bill invited me to go to New Orleans to Mardi Gras with him. After much deliberation, I accepted. It was 1981. After our arrival we learned that for the second time in the history of Mardi Gras, the famous annual event would be canceled. The police were striking, and the Mayor of New Orleans felt it was too unsafe to hold the event without police support. Despite the cancellation, we dined and danced in great fashion while we walked through the historic New Orleans French Quarter. Bill repeatedly veered me towards the jewelry shops. I sensed that he wanted to broach the subject of marriage, but I was not at that level with him. Bill was so kind, but it was the last thing on my mind.

On the plane back to Albany via Chicago, we sat three-to-a-row with a businessman in the third seat. Bill began to ply me with his marriage proposal. He asked where I'd like to go on our honeymoon, where I would like to live, and the sort of house I wanted. I tried to let him down gently, although I made no headway. Abruptly, the man sitting beside us with his head buried in the Wall Street Journal said, "Why don't you just give in and marry the guy?" I was stunned but responded just as suddenly, "Why don't you marry him and leave me out of this?" Then I hastily left for the loo.

While this took place, we had not noticed that passengers spoke in panicked voices and sounded concerned. Apparently, the landing gear failed to descend upon our approach to O'Hare Airport. When we saw an army of fire engines, police cars, flashing lights, and ambulances on the tarmac below, our attention piqued. The automatic mechanism for the landing gear did not engage, so we would land belly down. The co-pilot manually extended the wheels and prevented a devastating catastrophe, and that leg of the trip came to a safe conclusion. I disembarked the plane both safely and not engaged to Bill.

At the stopover at O'Hare, my Auntie Ann and my cousins, Marion and Linda, waited to welcome me for the short time we were on the ground. I knew they loved the idea of me dating a nice Jewish man, but I quietly explained that things just were not working romantically with Bill.

Stan Rubin was the conductor for the Canadian Symphony Orchestra and a Ph.D. in Music. After his divorce, Stan moved to Albany and was determined to establish an orchestra for the Capital City. He became my very dear friend.

Once Stan had arranged a superb group of musicians, which he called The Stan Rubin Orchestra, he needed both a theater and financing for promotion. He arranged and booked concerts with his new symphony. I helped him find materials to build a conductor's podium. It was fun to construct and pat ourselves on the back for our creations. I was excited for Stan and his new endeavors and wanted to see him succeed.

Stan taught me a great deal about music and the workings of symphony orchestras. Once, he invited Erin and me as his special guests to an upcoming concert. The piece he chose to dedicate to me was "Fanfare for the Common Man "by Aaron Copland. The piece was written in response to the United States entry into the Second World War and brought back many memories of wartime London. I had tears streaming, simultaneously happy and sad. What a grand evening it was. I was truly honored.

One evening, he called to tell me that he felt horrible and needed to go to the hospital. I gladly took him. His prognosis of multiple sclerosis left a hole in our hearts. Regardless, he continued with his dream of the Capital District Symphony Orchestra. Over the years I sadly lost touch with Stan. I will always hold my memories of him dearly.

I remained on crutches for far too long after my skiing accident. My knee wasn't healing properly. It did not stop me though and I went on with life full speed ahead. I attended a dance with the singles group. I was in pain and noticeably limping. An orthopedic doctor, Chuck, was also a member of our group and approached me at the dance and asked what I had done to my leg. I explained the skiing accident. I told him about the problems I had with my HMO. A physician's assistant had injected steroids in my knee, which moderated the pain, but caused further damage. I suppose that the injections reduced the pain to the point I was able to walk but did little to correct the underlying problem. Likely, Chuck thought that the treatment made my injury worse.

Chuck was angry on my behalf, and he gave me the name of a specialist in sports medicine at the Albany Medical Center. He insisted that I contact my HMO and use his name as a referral. Finally, I received the treatment that I needed, and the healing process began.

Despite meeting Chuck at a singles group event, I naively thought Chuck's interest was strictly professional, but his intentions were more romantically related. About ten years my junior at 37-years-old, Chuck had never married. His parents and his brother lived in Hollywood, California. His devotion to his domineering mother was overwhelming, however. He spoke with her on the telephone every day without a miss and she told him what to do and how to run his life. It was a strange relationship in my opinion.

Although Chuck could not join me, I had the opportunity to meet his parents. They lived close to my father who had recently moved to southern California. Because I really liked Chuck, I thought meeting his parents, even without Chuck along for the trip, would be a good idea.

He told his mother I would travel to see my family in southern California and wanted to meet her. Chuck's mother kindly invited my father, Brian and his wife, Yvonne, and their two children and me to dinner at her Hollywood home. The table was set with gorgeous silverware, china, and crystal. Chuck's mother apologized for not using her best tableware. She explained that with children joining the dinner party, she did not want to worry about anything getting broken. If that was not her best tableware, I was hard-pressed to imagine what was. As her cook was off for the day, she had the meal catered.

During dinner, the phone rang, and she left the table before hurriedly returning to say she had to leave immediately. Her horrified husband asked what was so urgent that she would not be able to finish dinner and entertain her guests. Apparently, a clothing store on Rodeo Drive was having a sale on a dress that she wanted, and she could not miss the chance for the bargain. Although our ideas of a bargain were quite different.

Her husband and son asked her to stay until the end of dinner. Dinner was barely over when she left the table and prepared to leave the house. She refused to wait for dessert and decided she would like me to accompany her on her mission. My sister-in-law Yvonne, who obviously knew that I was a single mother with two jobs, no money to speak of, and an empty checkbook, said, "Elaine, have you got your checkbook with you in case you find something for yourself?" I looked at Yvonne with daggers, but on the inside, I was actually laughing.

Chuck's mother made her purchase while I window shopped. I could not have even afforded a t-shirt, let alone anything else. Her new dress had to be carried by a guard to the cashier. After she paid for it, we were escorted to the door.

Before I left New York, Chuck had specifically told me not to tell his mother about my children. Stubbornly, I thought, I would not deny my children's existence to her or anyone. So, during the drive back to her home, Chuck's mother stopped at an open vegetable market. I think her real intention was to have a chance to learn more about me.

During our supposed informal chat, I subtly mentioned that while I was in California, I would make inquiries into colleges for my 17-year-old daughter Erin. She seemed astounded that I had a teenage child. I thought that as long as I was being completely honest, I would tell her about my son, Scott, who had finished college and was gainfully employed at Disney World in Orlando, Florida. Her shock was palpable. She called Chuck to express her horror that he was in love with a mother of two grown children.

Chuck met me at the airport in Albany and proceeded to give me an animated tongue-lashing. It was at that moment that I knew this relationship was doomed. A grown man who could not decide without help from his mother probably would not make a good partner. In addition, Chuck thought that he may want to have children of his own someday. There was little or no chance of that happening with me as his partner.

Not long after I returned from California, Chuck and I planned to attend a wine and cheese party given by a member of the singles group, but Chuck wasn't feeling well. I visited him with some chicken soup, as any good "Yiddisha" momma would do. He was rude and obnoxious, so I left and went to the party without him. That was the end of Chuck.

HOME ALONE

Not everything was going as well for me as I hoped it would. It seemed I was pulled in three directions, my need to be a mother, my need to make a living, and my need to be emotionally fulfilled as a woman. I was anything but peaceful and I experienced many sleepless nights and terrible sorrow that I was not being the mother I wanted to be to Erin. I suffered from migraine headaches and dreadful fatigue. I worried about Erin being alone at home after school. From the time Ron and I separated when Erin was 12-years old until the time she left home to attend college, she spent much of the time by herself or with friends about whom I felt unsure.

Ron was helpful to an extent, but he also had the same constraints as I did. After Mario Cuomo was elected as New York's governor, Ron took a position as Cuomo's Deputy Press Secretary, which taxed his time and his energy to a greater extent. Even so, when I was away from Clifton Park, such as during my California trip and other times I had to travel, Erin stayed with Ron and Carol. Those times eased my mind a bit.

An intelligent, creative, and thoughtful young lady, Erin hoped to pursue art and photography. She did well in high school, although she did not always attend classes. As many teenagers might have, Erin found ways to rebel and cutting class was one of the easier ways she could do that as there was no one home to see her off to the school bus.

With the ability to look back from where I sit today, I wish I would have made different decisions all those years ago. If I could go back and live that part of my life again, I would. Yes, I had to work to put food on the table and to pay the rent. However, I would have been home more for Erin and gone out less for me. I would have spent more time with Erin and guided her through the difficulties of adolescence and becoming a woman.

I am fortunate that my relationship with my daughter has been a close and loving one for nearly all the time she has been on this earth. I am also grateful that Erin's relationship with Ron is equally as strong, special, and loving today.

JERRY

After leaving Chuck, surly and rude, at his house with my chicken soup, I continued on to the party with my cheese and crackers. On the way, I ran into a man who was carrying a bottle of wine. He told me his name was Jerry, that he was also going to the party, and admitted that he was lost. I said, "I'm lost, too."

We finally arrived and once there I was greeted by friends and familiar faces. One of them, a man to whom I had never previously spoken, walked over to me. Without much ado, the man began to tell off-color jokes. I tried to move away, but the man followed me. Jerry was nearby, noticed my discomfort, and asked what I wanted to drink. When he returned with my soda, Jerry stood in between the man and me as though to dismiss him. Jerry and I talked briefly and, as the party dwindled, the two of us went our separate ways.

Our Halloween party was our next event. I dressed as medieval Lady Guinevere in a long white gown and cone shaped tulle covered hat. One of my dance partners was dressed as a teabag. He was covered from head to toe by a brown sack and a huge Lipton's Tea sign hung down by his side on a string. As we danced, he repeatedly asked me if I knew who he was. Later, he took off the brown sack and asked me to dance once again. I realized the Lipton Tea Bag was Jerry, my knight in shining armor from the previous party. He was there with a date. I did not give him my number, but he was able to subtly get it from a friend.

A short time later, Jerry and I met for a drink at The Cranberry Bog before my coat- check shift. When my friend, Jean, who was scheduled to work with me that night was not able to come in, Jerry stayed to help me. That was his second act of chivalry.

I learned from Jerry that he was an executive at the Combined Insurance Company that had offices across the street from the restaurant. While working as a coat-checker at The Cranberry Bog, any one of his employees or coworkers could have seen him, but that did not worry or phase him.

Jerry and I dated quite a bit. He was very attentive and romantic in his own way. We were quite attracted to one another, and our time spent together became more frequent. Jerry confessed he was falling in love with me. I was very fond of him at this point, and we became a confirmed and exclusive couple.

Technically, Jerry was still married, but legally separated and was in the process of divorce. Combined Insurance asked him to return to their headquarters in Chicago for a promotion to vice-president. Jerry wanted me to join him and start fresh in the Chicago suburbs, but I was hesitant. I did not want to leave Erin in New York during her senior year of high school, so I waited. When Erin graduated and started college in the fall, I would begin a new life with Jerry.

When Erin left Clifton Park to start her freshman year at SUNY Purchase, I left for Chicago. Ron and I took Erin to Purchase to move in and begin her four-year journey to her fine art degree. Immediately following, Jerry and I rented a U-Haul and began our journey to Illinois. During the trip, I felt some elation about starting a new life, however the majority of the time I felt unbearably unhappy and guilty about moving so far away from Erin. Yet, we continued onward to our new home in Lake Bluff, Illinois on the North Shore outside Chicago. The home was a dream, however the life surrounding would prove something else.

Once we arrived in Lake Bluff, my mixed emotions about my decision were far from resolved. Suddenly, Jerry became harsh, domineering, and rude. His generosity vanished as did the kind nature he had displayed in New York. He meanly picked apart everything I did and said. I unpacked and organized our new home. I hung artwork, arranged furniture and I was desperate for a feeling of being home in the new house and an unfamiliar part of the world. It was reminiscent of the move from London to Missouri decades earlier. However, this time, I wasn't surrounded by love and support.

Jerry took down all the pictures I had hung because the nails behind them did not match one another. He was extremely fastidious and "fixed" just about anything I touched. He threw the newspaper at me after we had been there for a week, and barked, "You're not here on a free ride, so get out and find a job." He insisted that I take the accumulated retirement benefits out of my New York State savings to buy myself a second-hand car so I could drive to whatever job I found.

I wondered what had happened to the man who had lovingly courted me in New York. Far from my loved ones and in a strange and new place, I once again sank into depression.

Jerry and I planned to get married a couple of months after our arrival in Chicago. After being there for a while with Jerry, however, I felt trapped and unsure whether making a commitment to this man in the form of marriage was the right thing to do. I had changed my entire life to be with Jerry and I hoped, once we married, my station would improve. I was hesitant but hopeful.

Midnight on the eve of our wedding, Jerry asked me to sign a prenuptial agreement. Shock did not even start to describe my reaction. Jerry had a year of courtship to discuss a prenuptial agreement with me. My family from England and California had already arrived as did Scott and Erin. Regardless, I refused to sign, and I told him that I would not marry him if both he had that little trust in me and had not had the character to discuss it prior to hours before the ceremony. Jerry backed down.

At this point and, perhaps, earlier, I had become very doubtful about following through with the marriage to Jerry. However, I believed, rightfully so, that I had jumped with both feet into the ocean, this new world and new life in Lake Bluff, without a life-preserver. I had ended my lease to the apartment in Clifton Park. I had resigned from my job. I had no source of income. I had believed Jerry was someone and something that he was not, but I felt like I did not have any choice. By that time, I am not sure that I did.

On Thanksgiving Day 1983, I married Jerry in a non-denominational church considering Jerry was Lutheran and I was an Edgar Caycean Jew. Dad had created a beautiful wedding dress for me and a gorgeous headpiece. Brian's wife, Yvonne, made a three-tier wedding cake and carefully transported it from Upland, California. My family from England, California, New York, and Florida as well as Jerry's children from Chicago and Minnesota joined us to celebrate the union. We wrote our vows, and the entire production went swimmingly, although Jerry's parents who lived nearby in Iowa did not attend. The idea of their son marrying outside his faith was abhorrent to them. Jerry was not surprised by their decision, but we were both disappointed.

The following day, we celebrated Thanksgiving before our loved ones all departed back to their respective homes and lives. Those two days were very special to me and I appreciated the love and support from my family, but I was sad to watch them leave. Then, there was just Jerry and me to start our lives as a married couple.

I tried to find happiness in my situation. As a girl, I had lived in strangers' homes without my parents and siblings and managed. As a young woman, I had moved to a new country and made the best of it. I could do it again. Jerry and I lived in a lovely home, my Auntie Anne and my cousins lived in nearby Des Plaines, Illinois, and I found work once again as a Kelly Girl.

The jobs that followed as a Kelly Girl did not turn out to be good fits for me. I was not able to find my niche and often regretted leaving my interesting and rewarding work in Marty Solomon's office and the New York State Senate.

I took a position at an Allstate Insurance headquarters office in suburban Chicago and worked as an assistant for two corporate attorneys there. At first, the work seemed to be a fit, but because I was so unhappy at home, I cried much of the time and could not focus on what could have been enjoyable and rewarding work. It was horrible to be far away from my children and Jerry showed no compassion. He was cold and unsupportive. He seemed incapable of empathy.

Jerry was an extremely difficult man. In contrast to the man he had shown me to be when he worked with me at The Cranberry Bog, the reality was that Jerry demonstrated that he was cold, unsupportive, and often disrespectful towards me. When I tried to speak with him about my concerns with his demeanor, he simply said, "If you do not like it, you can move out." Of course, he knew I had no means to start my life over again, yet he dared me to go. If I cried openly, he held his newspaper up in front of his face to show he didn't care at all and then left the room with a slam of the door. He seemed to enjoy the power he had over me and I blamed myself that I gave it to him. I felt the familiar feeling of depression and being alone, but I knew I had to find my strength as I had done many times in my past.

DOOR COUNTY

About a year after Jerry and I married, we bought a cottage situated on the banks of Lake Michigan in Wisconsin's picturesque Door County. Shortly thereafter, we purchased another cottage in nearby Sister Bay. I enjoyed designing and decorating on a budget, which had always been a passion of mine. These two cottages were great for my mental health and a saving grace to me during the early years of our difficult marriage. I had a creative outlet and something to occupy my mind that I genuinely enjoyed. Jerry and I remodeled the house in Door County. I painted the walls white to brighten the cathedral ceilings and decorated it with a nautical theme to compliment the lakeside environment. We rented it to summer residents for a few years and sold it at a nice profit. This allowed us to build a whole new addition onto our second cottage in Sister Bay.

The Sister Bay cottage was older and needed a lot of tender loving care. I installed a beautiful ceramic tile counter in the kitchen, painted the dark wood panels white, helped Jerry build a larger deck, and cleaned up the stony beach so we could enjoy our little retreat.

Our Thursday routine in Lake Bluff included packing our bags, so on Friday we could leave immediately after work to relax at the Sister Bay cottage. Our little slice of heaven was a five-hour drive. We would stop outside of Milwaukee for dinner then head straight for the shore. I found creative ways to brighten the rooms, bought home furnishings, and tidied the external space. I found this was therapeutic and lightened my spirit. Without this regular retreat to look forward to all week, I surely would not have survived the marriage. Door County was a beautiful place to nurse my wounds and heal.

Cycling was popular among the residents of Door County. Jerry, himself, was a dedicated rider. Each year many of these cyclists met at the ferry dock in Ellison Bay and rode the ferry with bikes in tow to Washington Island. The island was fertile ground for riding enthusiasts. I did not bike, myself, so I became the driver of the SAG (support and gear) wagon for the whole gang. I followed them over the entire island in my car to help repair broken bikes, provide hydration, or apply bandages. We stopped at every little cafe, restaurant, and bar on the tiny island to eat, drink, freshen up, and rest before we would set off on our adventures again. We would leave on the last ferry home and watch the colorful, glorious sunset as we crossed Lake Michigan. These times soothed my soul and nothing at the time could have been better for Jerry and me.

Scott was rarely able to escape his executive duties at Disney World in Orlando, Florida for a vacation. He visited us a few times and it was always a joy to me. For Scott, he was able to relax in the quiet countryside as the waves rolled in on beautiful Lake Michigan. Jerry's son, Scott, and Erin often joined us during their summer breaks from college. We would spend entire weeks together at the cottage and enjoy games, hikes, good food, and laughter. The cottage proved to be a wonderful retreat for our family.

One morning, we heard a loud scratching at our front door, and we all went outside to investigate. The adorable clawing creature was a young racoon. We approached it cautiously and it did not flinch. It came closer and rubbed right against Erin's legs. This masked and dexterous animal seemed to be tame. Erin cut an apple and we were amazed when it crawled up her leg to gently grab it from her hand. It was so docile and unafraid. Erin took a glass of milk to the raccoon, and we watched as it drank out of the glass like a little person. We concluded that this raccoon had been someone's pet. We did not dare let it inside, so it nestled on the roof near the chimney and slept there each night. We named it "Baby" and it followed us on walks in the woods and along the stony beach as if it were a dog.

By weeks' end, we prepared to return home to Lake Bluff, but worried about Baby who seemed reliant on our affection and small offerings of food. Erin escorted the small raccoon deep into the woods in hopes that it would adapt to the natural habitat throughout the week. When Erin reached the road on her return, she turned and quietly called "Baby" as a test. Within moments the critter was at her heels again. Months later, when we visited Door County again, we went to the woods edge and called for Baby. To our amazement, Baby appeared and greeted us. Thankfully, she appeared healthy.

Jerry's friends in Door County were simply wonderful and welcomed me into their lives with open arms. We met for many gatherings, like yacht club cruises, pancake breakfasts, birthday dinners, Sister Bay parades, art shows, and fish boils on our beach for Independence Day each year.

Early settlers from Scandinavian countries brought the tradition of fish boils with them to the Upper Great Lakes region. The ingredients are simple and include fish, potatoes, onions, and salt. Many of the settlers were fishermen and outdoor living was their style. Whitefish were easy to find in the lakes, vegetables were simple to grow in the rich soil, and outdoor cooking was not a hardship. We had a 50-gallon cauldron in which we added tiny, peeled onions, baby potatoes and salt to the boiling pot. We created a large bonfire on the beach and placed the cauldron on the fire to heat. We let the vegetables cook then we placed fresh fish from Lake Michigan onto the top rack of the steaming cauldron. As we stood and watched, a small kettle of kerosene was thrown onto the fire which caused a blaze of flames to cover the top of the pot and burn off the fish scales quickly. We were cautious with the kerosene lest our eyebrows could be singed off, or worse. I never forgot my mother in wartime burning off her eyebrows with our potbelly stove.

When the fire was doused there were cheers all around and a feast to follow. Everyone contributed to the festivities and brought salad, buns, beverages, and desserts. Tables along our beach were filled with friends and laughter. We ate, joked, and enjoyed one another's company.

After the first few years of our fish boils, I started to add tiny carrots to the pot, against tradition. I earned a nickname for my efforts and for many years, everyone called me "Carrots."

MISS-ADVENTURE

Jerry and I bought an old motorboat to further enjoy our time at the lake. It was not, by any means, under warranty and often stalled. Among the experienced mariners in our group, the motorboat earned the moniker, "Stink Pot." People who did not use the wind to ride the currents were considered curious. However, our boat got much use, and light-hearted derision from everyone.

On one occasion, we took our friend John on a ride on Stink Pot. After a short cruise on Lake Michigan, we docked at Bailey's Harbor. As we approached the dock, John took the rope and threw it lasso style to reach the mooring post. Jerry was moving a bit too fast and we overshot our destination. The boat hit the dock, flew up, and landed on top of the dock rather than beside it. We climbed out of the boat and jumped down. Other boaters who had seen the debacle came to assist us. Together we pushed Stink Pot back into the water, properly docked. Thankfully, nothing but our egos were bruised. We bought the lettering for the boat right then at the harbor store and changed her name to "Miss-Adventure."

On another occasion, Jerry and I had Miss-Adventure on the lake. Curiously, there were no other boats out that day. That should have been a signal that something was amiss, but we continued to a small inlet where we enjoyed lunch at a tiny cafe. As we left the cafe to head for home, we noticed clouds had formed overhead. The water began to swell and the boat rocked back and forth. Suddenly, the sky opened with a violent thunderstorm. Jerry had experience sailing a boat, but motoring was a lot different. Each time he headed into a wave, we got soaked. We were dreadfully unprepared for such circumstances. We tried to hug the shoreline, but it was too jagged, and the waves repeatedly swept us towards the dangerous rocks.

Fighting to stay upright against the lashing rain and powerful waves, we looked for a safe place to dock. Our home dock at Bailey's Harbor was too far. After three hours, we finally decided to beach Miss-Adventure. We struggled to secure the boat so it wouldn't drift away in the storm, but we finally did. Only later when we were dried off and warmed up did we admit to each other how scared we had been. We never ventured that far away again unless we checked the weather before any journey.

One weekend, Jerry's daughter, JoAnn, her husband, Barry and their four-year old daughter, Sarah, visited us at the cottage. Jerry and I were excited to show them Miss-Adventure. Sarah decided to voyage with us to provide JoAnn and Barry some time alone. The three of us boarded Miss-Adventure and motored away from Bailey's Harbor while Sarah's parents stood on the dock waving and wishing us, "Bon voyage."

When Miss-Adventure was out of sight of the dock and the waving had stopped, so did the motor. Jerry's granddaughter was nervous and started to cry. As I held her in my arms, I told her that we were on a special adventure and there was nothing to worry about. I said this voyage was to be put in a storybook for children. She brightened a bit, while we waited to wave down anyone who happened to pass. After some time, a passing boat saw our plight and arranged for a tow back to Bailey's Harbor. Later, Jerry and I cheerily joked about the apropos name we had chosen for the boat, but JoAnn and Barry didn't see the humor.

Miss-Adventure had certainly given us our fair share of frustration. Like many things in life, Jerry and I put up with the trials of that boat as long as she gave us more joy than trouble. Once that balance tilted, we bid farewell to our Miss-Adventure and sold it to someone who could make her more seaworthy.

Gloria and Ray enjoyed their visits to picturesque Sister Bay. The two had started to look for a cottage of their own. Around 1990, they bought a property on the same road as our cottage and began to use it as their summer home. It was such a joy to have them so close to us. While my station and my emotional health had improved a great deal since those first few months of marriage, my happiest times were spent in Sister Bay where Jerry was under less stress. During the times he and I spent in Lake Bluff, Jerry continued to be overbearing, harsh, and demeaning toward me. With Gloria nearby, often during our times at the cottage however, I felt a sense of respite. Once again, I felt Gloria and Ray had, in many ways, rescued me as they had done so many times in my life.

The cottage Gloria and Ray bought had a small beach and was surrounded by trees and brush. The house had been set up as a kind of dorm. Mattresses had been tucked into every nook and cranny. The cottage was also not terribly well constructed and was in dire need of tender loving care. At the same time, it had great potential and, with a bit of imagination, Gloria and I knew, it would become a beautiful second home.

So, the four of us had a project. We started by renting a trailer we hitched to Jerry's car. Jerry and Ray hauled away stacks of mattresses for what seemed like days while Gloria and I started on the inside of the house cleaning and making small repairs. As Jerry and Ray cut trees and cleared brush revealing a breathtaking view of Lake Michigan, Gloria and I shopped at garage sales, thrift shops, and flea markets for bargains on everything from furniture to dishware. Like our father was, Gloria is a talented seamstress and she reupholstered old couches and chairs and created handsome curtains. Although painstakingly exhausting, our efforts were rewarding and enjoyable. As important to me as anything else, Jerry and I worked together and accomplished something meaningful. Although a small step, I believe it was an important one to help create some respect from Jerry for me. At least as important, I spent time with Gloria and that made me happy.

Throughout our work that summer, friends stopped to check our progress. Often, those friends joined us for drinks and food at our cottage or we would all go to a restaurant for good conversation, good food, and good friendship. Finally, our work had finished, and Gloria and Ray had a home they could enjoy while I would relish having my sister close to me much more frequently.

HIT AND RUN

During my first years living on the North Shore of Chicago, I made a monthly visit to my Auntie Anne, and my first cousin, Marion. I would also meet Marion after work on occasion for dinner and share all the family news. Marion's life had been a difficult journey. Her husband, Joe, was often ill and had major heart complications, which plunged him into deep depression. In true London cockney fashion, Joe masked his troubles with humor and was always a joy to be around, despite his condition.

On a stormy New Year's Eve in 1993, Marion visited Joe in the intensive care unit of a hospital in Chicago after he suffered a heart attack. Marion's daughter, Marcia, happened to be an emergency room nurse at the same hospital. Marion left the hospital when visiting hours ended at eight o'clock to meet her sons, Graham and Simon, for dinner to discuss how their dad was recovering. On her way to dinner, Marion was struck by a speeding vehicle that raced through the crosswalk where she was crossing adjacent to the hospital. The driver of the vehicle did not stop and, after Marion lay on the pavement for some time, a pedestrian discovered her and ran into the emergency room to get help. We never learned whether Marion was killed immediately by the driver or whether she lived for some time after being struck. Regardless, my dear cousin passed away that night.

When Marion's daughter, Marcia, arrived at the emergency room to work that night, she did not immediately know that the gurney holding the deceased body covered with a sheet in one of the rooms was that of her mother. When a doctor identified the body and told her that her Mum had died, Marcia went into shock. Neither Marcia, nor the hospital staff knew how to break the news to Joe in the intensive-care unit, that his wife had been killed shortly after her visit with him.

The nightly news on New Year's Eve covered the stark scene of the empty street crossing where just one shoe lay in the road. When Marcia called to tell me the victim of the hit-and-run was Marion, I was shaken to my core knowing my dear cousin was gone. Marion had survived a war but was killed crossing a Chicago street.

The following day a woman came forth and admitted to being the negligent driver. She was sentenced to merely six weeks of community service. I attended the hearing and was appalled when she rolled her eyes to the courthouse ceiling as if the punishment was unjust. She did not apologize nor offer condolences to the family whose lives she destroyed. I had learned very young in my life that some losses were not connected to reason. I was reminded to treasure each moment as we do not know which breath will be our last.

ERIN

I was gratified to know that Erin was thriving. She had graduated from SUNY-Purchase with a Bachelor of Fine Arts. SUNY-Purchase is still known for its arts, dance and theater programs and among Erin's classmates were Stanley Tucci, Edie Falco, Wesley Snipes, and Brooke Smith, among others. While not a film actor, Erin experienced recognition as an artist and showed at galleries throughout the Northeast including Square One Gallery on Block Island, Rhode Island, Tower Gallery in Port Chester, New York, and The Neuberger Museum in Purchase, New York.

Chris Clark was a pilot in Kenya for the American Committee for the Red Cross and UNICEF. He flew aid workers throughout Kenya, Tanzania, and Somalia. He helped transport aid to African villages to people in need. It was quite dangerous work as some among the recipients were, in fact, hijackers who commandeered planes after the payload was delivered. They were desperate people. During his needed breaks from this stressful job, Chris would visit his sister in New York. On one of those holidays, Chris met Erin, who was a friend of Chris's sister Tina.

A courtship ensued and spanned two continents. Soon after they met, Erin moved to Kenya to live with Chris. In Africa, Erin and Chris took exotic safaris and made a life within a compound of expatriates. It was an election year in Kenya and the capital city of Nairobi was turbulent. The political atmosphere in Kenya bears little resemblance to that in England or the United States. Voter disenfranchisement and fraud often creates a violent and dangerous undercurrent where no one is safe. Although living overseas was exciting and captivating, a real danger existed for Kenyan nationals and foreign workers alike. Given the circumstances, Erin and Chris mutually decided to return to the safety of the United States not just for their sake, but also for that of my unborn grandchild.

Erin and Chris relocated to Santa Fe, New Mexico into a beautiful adobe house with brick paved floors, adobe Kiva fireplaces in each room, and windows overlooking an arroyo surrounded by rugged desert hills. Chris's father had built a massive home for his children to reside in if they were ever in need. He was a talented architect who studied under Frank Lloyd Wright. The home beautifully mirrored the lines of the New Mexican high desert landscape in its shape and color. Stunning views and sunsets surrounded the abode. Half of the of the property was rented to tenants and the two sides of the home were kept private from the other by a gorgeous hand carved wooden door.

Erin was grateful to be stateside to have their first child in a safe environment, but she and Chris needed work to afford their new life. Chris found a job as a corporate Learjet pilot in New York while Erin remained in Santa Fe until their son was born. I joined her as her due date approached to keep her and her new Labrador puppy, Cosmo, company.

While Erin was at her job at a fine arts printing facility, New Media Arts, I stayed home with Cosmo. After Erin returned home from work one afternoon, Cosmo escaped from the house to investigate the freshly fallen snow. The two of us ran outside in our slippers without coats and keys as the door to the house slammed closed and locked behind us. Domestic animals are a favorite snack of the local coyote population. Not minding the cold, Cosmo jumped about having great fun. We, on the other hand, were freezing. Erin was big-bellied by then and couldn't see her feet. The focus of our efforts transitioned from collecting Cosmo to getting back into the house. We tried windows, which were locked against the frigid mountain air. Around the house we went to try to find a way inside. We noticed John, the home's tenant, was leaving for work and spoke with him before he got in his car. John generously let us stay on his side of the house, with his three-legged dog, Pogo, and three-legged cat, Pie.

The massive, wooden door separating the two residences was the only way back into our side. It was bolted shut from the other side. Erin located a few tools in the tenants' toolbox, while I found a ladder. Erin and her big belly climbed the ladder to the hinges. After struggling, she managed to push out the hinge bolts and we struggled to move the door aside and Erin squeezed through to our side of the house followed by me and Cosmo who wagged his tail, happy to be home. Pogo and Pie tried fruitlessly to follow.

For medical reasons, Erin's doctors made the decision to induce labor. Chris returned two days before the planned delivery, and he drove Erin and me through the Sante Fe desert to St. Vincent's Hospital. I remember snowflakes gently falling on that April morning. To keep my mind occupied and distracted from the thought of Erin enduring what could be a difficult childbirth, I brought my sewing kit with me. I was making a teddy bear for Erin's best friend, Su, who was also about to give birth to her first child more than 2,000-miles away in The Bronx. As I waited in the delivery room, I created the teddy bear that had two legs and two arms that pointed in the wrong direction.

Cooper was born that day, April 13, 1998. I was elated to meet my first grandchild. Both Erin and Cooper were healthy, and the birth had gone well. Cooper was a beautiful baby and radiated with a bright light in my eyes. I was reluctant to return to Lake Bluff both because of the struggles I often experienced with Jerry there and because I wanted to help my child during the first few months of having her own child. However, I had already been away for two months, and Jerry wanted me to return home. Eleven days after the delivery, Erin, Chris, and Cooper left Santa Fe for New York and new adventures. With strong, mixed feelings, I said, "Good-bye" to Erin and Cooper and boarded a flight destined for O'Hare International Airport and my life there.

MAID TO REMEMBER

The spiritual aura of Santa Fe combined with the birth of my first grandchild gave me a new sense of purpose. Between Jerry's occasionally explosive episodes and my work at Allstate Insurance, my life in Lake Bluff often contributed to my recurring depression. The other assistants supported only one attorney each, while I worked for two lawyers. I was drowning in an ocean of work. The other assistants painted their nails or made personal calls while I struggled to keep up with the demands of my very busy counselors.

I told Jerry I could not continue working each day in what I considered an unhealthy work environment. It came as no surprise that Jerry was unsupportive for, in my opinion, all the wrong reasons. As his wife, Jerry could easily have included me on Combined Insurance Company's health benefit plan, but he insisted I have my own. With my new resolve, I knew the environment at that Allstate Insurance office was not right for me. So, after five years, I made the decision to seek greener pastures.

Considering I was unemployed, Jerry suggested that I start my own business. As I was always cleaning and my home was usually spotless, he proposed that I start a maid service, but I really had no experience as an entrepreneur. So, I enrolled in an entrepreneur seminar in Atlanta, Georgia where I learned how to set up the business, studied methods to efficiently clean houses, and learned how to train and manage employees. When I returned to Lake Bluff, I founded Maid to Remember.

I hired several employees, and it seemed as though I was constantly training a new face. I discovered that many of the employees did not want to work. They wanted to have a job reference in order to claim unemployment benefits. Most did a lackluster job. It was common to get a call each afternoon with a complaint from a client. I would have to stop whatever I was doing to clean a four or five-bedroom house from top to bottom until late in the evening to please a customer. Some customers put coins behind doors so they could tell if it had been vacuumed. I would place each coin on the nearest dresser or table. I found this humiliating. I never made a profit in my business venture; it was a disaster.

My health had been deteriorating for some time. I was not physically fit for this line of work although I stuck it out for a year. Jerry got very worried at one point. He sent for my daughter Erin and bought her a plane ticket. After spending some time together, she told Jerry that if the situation went any further, I would likely have a nervous breakdown. She saw that both my body and mind had significantly declined since her last visit. It was a wake-up call.

I made the decision to dissolve my company. I chose my favorite four clients and I worked for them exclusively. This removed a huge burden as I no longer relied on the poor work ethics of others. After a few hours of work, many would offer me a cup of tea and invite me to relax and chat. It was enriching to have great relationships with my customers. I did not feel belittled anymore and I enjoyed doing a proper job. Although I had only four homes to clean, I was still not in the physical shape needed to do this type of work. It took its toll.

WHY NOT ME

After I told my clients that I would no longer be working, and given my dubious relationship with Jerry, I was anxious and uncertain about my future. I felt that I needed to be able to take care of myself. Overwhelmed and exhausted, I generally felt unwell. I would soon discover that it was not just my angst about a career change that was the reason for lethargy.

I made the time to visit a doctor and was diagnosed with breast cancer.. I would have to undergo a quadrantectomy, which would remove the cancer but preserve my breast. Gloria and Erin came to Chicago to help me both practically, with groceries, cooking, and rides to and from my appointments and emotionally, as I faced a breast cancer diagnosis.

Before the surgery, the three of us took a short holiday to Door County and stayed at our cottage on the beach. I knew this would be therapeutic for me as I approached my upcoming surgery. The gentle waves of Lake Michigan and the company of my sister and my daughter could not have been better medicine.

During this time, Jerry was not only distracted with his management responsibilities at Combined Insurance, but he was also taking classes at night to get a real estate license. He had planned to be a real estate agent after his retirement from Combined Insurance. Jerry seemed to be preoccupied with everything or anything, but me. The evening of my surgery, Jerry had the final exam for the real estate license. I waited to see him after surgery. I was naturally anxious and needed comfort. After he had completed his exam, Jerry went on to a celebration party with the other students. The aching pain I felt that night was as much for a broken heart as much as I felt was for the cancer that was removed from my breast.

During my recovery, I learned the cancer was not completely removed and a partial mastectomy would be necessary. The trip to Door County had soothed my spirits so I could better face the upcoming months of worry and fear. Erin and Gloria had been lovingly supporting but needed to return to their own lives and responsibilities, which meant Jerry remained as my only support. The day I had been scheduled for the second surgery, he dropped me off at the Highland Park Hospital and left for work. I was unsurprised by his behavior but was not unaffected by it. I missed terribly the nurturing support of Gloria and Erin.

After the surgery, Jerry, of course, went to the office as if it was just another day. He had hoped that the hospital would send a nurse to empty the surgical tubes and exercise my arm. Jerry showed no interest to help in my recovery. Eventually, he did help me empty my post-surgical drainage tubes before and after he worked but would not take a day off. He told me that he had not taken a sick or personal day and wanted to keep that record so that he would get recognition for it when he retired.

A cancer support case worker made a visit to see me. She told me about an organization known as, "Why Me?" My first reaction was, "This sounds like a feel-sorry-for-yourself group." After all, "Why not me?" I respectfully declined the invitation.

During my first week of radiation treatment, a kind friend took me to the hospital each day. The following week, I got a ride with a neighbor who was also undergoing radiation treatments. For the remaining four weeks, I drove myself, which was a painful thing to endure both physically and psychologically. After six weeks of radiation, I did join another support group, but found it depressing. Hearing descriptions of life as a cancer victim did nothing to give me hope or cheer, so I soon quit.

Throughout, it was clear to me that Jerry simply did not share the same values of care and concern for others that I always tried to extend. I treated strangers more warmly than Jerry treated me. Jerry's indifference did not help my state of mind. I was repeatedly caught off guard and sickened by his lack of empathy.

IN-LAWS

My radiation appointments were scheduled on mornings, Monday through Friday, so Jerry and I were still able to travel to Door County on weekends. I found great solace and spiritual healing in the nourishing environment at our cottage. My mental outlook improved noticeably in my peaceful space at Sister Bay and I was thankful for these opportunities. On the other hand, Jerry and I made trips to Ames, Iowa to see his parents. These visits to the Hawkeye State were something less so.

Jerry's parents were nonagenarians by then and quite settled in their ways. His father, Walter, was a kind natured gentleman and always welcoming. As if to prove the rule that opposites attract, Alice, Jerry's mother, was quite a tyrant. If we did not arrive exactly at the time Jerry told her we would after a 10-hour drive from Lake Bluff, she cursed and belittled us both. If Jerry's slacks were wrinkled or shoes were not shined, Alice scolded him callously. Even if there was nothing else with which to find fault, Alice brooded and scowled from the time we would arrive until the time we started our drive back home.

Once, when we visited Walter and Alice, Jerry asked me to record using a handheld video camera as he interviewed them about their lives. He wanted to document his family history and share it with the generations. Alice's reaction was as expected and was adamant about me not pointing the camera at her during the interview. She fought and fussed until she began to retreat as she heard Walter recount family stories in his gentle soft-spoken manner. Slowly, Jerry got them both to speak deeply about their past, she forgot I was filming, and I was able to capture them both sharing history.

If the trips to Ames were not spiritually enriching for me, they certainly helped me to understand Jerry's behavior a bit. While it was obvious to me that Jerry's disposition was learned and reinforced by his mother, I believe Jerry could have and each of us can make a conscious choice under any circumstance. Regardless of the difficulties we suffer, whether a mistreatment by others, a fate that bridles us with illness, or anything else, we can choose to be kind to one another.

SANIBEL RETIREMENT

In the early Nineties, Jerry and I bought a time-share on Sanibel Island where we vacationed for two weeks every January. We loved the shell-speckled, sandy beaches and natural beauty of the Gulf Coast. The time we spent there was as emotionally fulfilling for me as our cottage in Sister Bay.

We found a house situated on a canal that intersected the Gulf of Mexico. Although it had fallen into disrepair, the property had grand potential both due to its location and structural features. The house had been foreclosed and vacant for two years. The previous owner was the architect and builder of the home and in his dissatisfaction with the foreclosure process, dismantled all the electrical and plumbing fixtures. He removed a staircase, the air conditioning system, and, literally, the kitchen sink. A plague of translucent, white frogs had made home in the toilets and large, native snakes crawled along the exterior walls of the house. In short, it was the perfect project and we purchased the property in short-sale.

We asked for reinforcements for the reclamation and, once again, Gloria and Ray came to our aid. On this occasion, Scott also joined the team. We inflated air mattresses and slept on the floor in the unbearable heat of the Florida summer. We had purchased a steel spiral staircase at an ironworks in a small town in Indiana on our drive to Florida. Until Ray and Jerry installed it, we had never seen the upper loft. It was a generous, airy space with beautiful built-in shelving. There were 12-foot-wide sliding glass doors which led to an extensive deck that overlooked the canal. We worked tirelessly to install fixtures and appliances and finish all the fine details. It was a great project, and we had many laughs while fixing our future residence.

After we finished the "canal" house renovations and rented it while we planned for our retirement, Jerry decided to invest in a townhouse on a golf course on Sanibel Island. The property was nestled between the fifth tee and a small pond where the alligators basked. We renovated the property and quickly rented it. Unfortunately, our new tenants were hell-raisers who used the walls as dartboards, made countless burns on the carpets, the front door was torn from its hinges, and somehow disabled all but one burner and the oven on the brand-new stove. A parrot had run of the place and had left droppings, literally, everywhere. The local police were very familiar with the address considering neighbors had made many reports of the rowdy parties.

Upon Jerry's retirement, we evicted the tenants and moved into the townhouse ourselves. Although we enjoyed living on the golf course, we yearned to be on the water. So, after spending a year restoring the townhouse, Jerry and I rented it again and we moved into our dream home on the canal.

We had a raised boat dock installed on the canal to accommodate our new 23-foot sleeper motorboat. The boat was a life changer. We had some boating experience from our little Miss-Adventure boat in Lake Michigan, but we agreed it was vital to become more proficient with our boating knowledge considering we'd now cruise on ocean tides.

Jerry and I joined the Sanibel-Captiva Power Squadron where we took dozens of courses to improve our knowledge of the sea and boating. Jerry became a good captain, and I enjoyed being the captain's mate and whatever else it took to stay afloat. In one lesson, the instructor asked, "What would you do if the captain fell overboard?"

My immediate and naughty answer was "Throw him the anchor." Jerry did not appreciate the humor.

The Power Squadron took various overnight journeys that took us to the Everglades, Lake Okeechobee, Cabbage Key, Pine Island, and the botanical gardens of Useppa Island. The winding sandy pathways and unique homes were magical, lined with tiny fairy lights and lush tropical vegetation on Useppa. Exotic tropical trees and vibrant flowering plants dappled each nook and cranny of the landscape. The aroma was scrumptious. No motor vehicles were driven on the island and the transportation consisted of golf carts, bikes, or one's own two feet. The atmosphere was peaceful and soothing with magnificent sights and the fresh scent of the sea air and fragrant blooms. We ate like royalty and after dinner we would softly play our boat radios. Couples would dreamily sway in unison on the docks.

We awoke one morning to quite a shock at our canal home. I got up out of bed to let our little poodle out through the screened in pool area. Much to my surprise, lounging in our swimming pool was a nine-foot alligator. I quickly scooped up the little pup and yelled to Jerry to come quickly. He rushed out and saw me in shock staring at the gator in the pool. This was scary new territory to us. We called the police and they arrived almost immediately. They were equipped with large lassoes for these common occurrences.

Watching this huge creature fight four policemen showed us the strength of the reptile. It twisted and turned rather violently each time the noose surrounded any part of its body. It fought valiantly with its powerful tail and thrashed about trying to keep its captors at bay. The authorities were successful in their pursuit. They hauled the giant reptile out of the blue pool water onto the tiled deck. The gator was carefully escorted onto our front lawn. They dragged the heavy beast to a swampy ditch and released it. I shot a video of the exciting event and sent it to Animal Planet. A small clip was aired. They sent me $100.00 and an Animal Planet T-shirt large enough to fit the alligator.

One of my favorite sea animals that frequented our dock was the West Indian manatee. She was accompanied by her placid calf. I was intent on capturing the manatees on video, so I lay face down on our dock with my video camera in hand. I waited patiently as this majestic sea giant swam up to my face repeatedly to graze my nose. She and her young calf dove to the bottom of the clear canal water. After five minutes she would rise for a quick breath, a kiss on my nose and playfully take another deep dive. Manatees are gentle and social creatures that love to investigate their surroundings. The cow's curiosity and fearlessness were magical. I was blessed to experience this unusual interaction and capture it on video.

A large iguana lived on our property and seemed somewhat tame. She would approach me and skim her face on my camera lens. I named her Iggy. Every day, Iggy helped herself to the blooms from my lovingly planted flowers. I found her prehistoric features and slow movements quite fascinating. One unusually cold morning, Iggy lay in the yard completely still. She appeared to have died. Hours went by with no sign of movement and I was quite concerned. I called the local wildlife center and explained the situation. They could examine her only if I brought her to their center as iguanas are not native to Sanibel Island.

I had no assistance to lift the heavy reptile off the ground. I put some old beach towels in the dryer to heat them up and covered Iggy. I hoped this would give her warmth, if that was what was needed. The towels did not move from their position for two hours. Suddenly, I watched her bumpy face appear from under the beach towel. Iggy slowly revealed her four-foot-long torso and tail from under the warm towels. Thankfully, the cure was heat. I felt triumphant having given this creature the comfort it needed. Months later as I was taking a morning stroll, I spotted Iggy and two baby iguanas on a thick tree branch overhanging the canal. Iggy and her offspring remained on our property for many years.

UNCLE SYD

My Dad's brother, Syd, moved to a nursing home in Indiana with his wife, Cricket, who died a short time later. A dear English gentleman, Syd's heart broke when Cricket passed and, having no children of his own, became terribly lonesome. As much as we could, Jerry and I would visit Uncle Syd and were always warmly welcomed.

Tragically, Syd received an Alzheimer's diagnosis. We arranged to bring him to Florida to live with us, but we soon realized that our home was not a safe environment for Syd's rapidly progressing disease. I became his healthcare proxy and researched many facilities that specialized in his needs.

I located a reputable Alzheimer's facility in Fort Myers, a short drive from our home. The staff were experts in caring for patients with Alzheimer's and seemed compassionate. They took the time to stop and laugh with him and kiss the top of his head each time they passed his room. He remained delightful and light-hearted, even when faced with his illness. I visited him almost every day. He loved to go out to eat or have a picnic at a park nearby. It was such a treat for me to experience his joy and companionship. I felt fortunate that he knew who I was and could reminisce about our family and times gone by. He loved to sing with me, and his joy was infectious. When I'd leave him, he would struggle to escape through the garden gate to follow me. It was unbearable to watch as his joy turned to despair.

It was difficult when I left him for three weeks to see family in England. I arranged with various friends and Gloria to visit him as often as possible. Gloria was saddened when he did not recognize her at all. I was genuinely concerned about him and found it difficult to relax while I was in London. I returned from my trip and decided to pop in for a visit before returning home. On my drive from Fort Myers Airport to the nursing home I received the phone call that he had just taken his last breath. They assured me he had died peacefully without a struggle. My heart ached.

IN SIGHT OF AMERICA

Over the years I was fortunate to have the means to travel quite extensively. These experiences guided me to look outward with a renewed sense of wonder and celebration of the natural world surrounding us. As a young girl in London, I had dreamt of traveling after the enriching experiences spent on the English seaside. I will forever carry all of these sights and adventures with me.

The time we spent in New Mexico was otherworldly. I was astounded with the stalagmites and stalactites formed over millions of years at Carlsbad Caverns. Santa Fe was a magical artist's world rich with color and inspiration. The Sangre de Cristo Mountain Range was breathtaking with snowy peaks towering at 13,000 feet. We saw herds of majestic pronghorn antelope, packs of swift coyotes, long eared black-tailed jack rabbits and the shiny silver leaves of the aspen trees. The scenery was surreal with pink adobe homes speckling the sparse high desert landscape and contrasting with brilliant blue skies. Native American reservations were scattered throughout the state and were jarring. The poverty was evident with crowded living conditions and inadequate plumbing. Looking into the sunken, hollow eyes of the children and the despondent faces of the mother and fathers, I felt a need to help. Although the reality was clear, there was nothing productive that I could accomplish.

Mount Rushmore National Memorial in Black Hills South Dakota was a majestic sight. The mountain carvings were true to the likenesses of the four United States Presidents they represent. The granite faces are 60-feet tall. Originally the carvings were to include the details to each President's waist, however insufficient funding left us with only their heads. It was fascinating to imagine the years of grueling work from 1927-1941 that went into creating this mountain sculpture. I shuddered at the danger the men faced who created this magnificent wonder so high in the mountaintops.

The Hoover Dam was a spectacular feat of brilliant engineering. The massive hydro-electric power plant was built in the Colorado River between the border of Arizona and Nevada to provide irrigation water and control flooding. It was constructed during the great depression by thousands of workers. This once in a lifetime experience was worth the boat cruise on the picturesque Lake Mead in the 110-degree weather.

It was a rare treat to visit Yellowstone National Park in Wyoming. The extraordinary gush of Old Faithful left us breathless as it climbed over 100-feet into the sky. We watched American bison walking the riverbeds, grizzly bears sauntering by our car making my heart beat quickly, and elk herds grazing on the unspoiled prairie. We drove through the park four times in four days to be sure we saw as much as possible. The wildlife, natural springs, and stunning landscape left an impression on me that will last my lifetime.

The Grand Canyon made me gasp in disbelief and wonder. The view of its 1,904 square miles carved some 6 million years ago is truly a wonder of our world. We learned of the native tribes that resided in the nooks and crannies of the caves. I admired their resilience and stamina living through the daily weather changes, hunting for food and existing in the deep caverns. We witnessed a sunset that raged a fiery red and gradually calmed into soft blue and purple hues until indigo darkness filled the vast canyon.

I felt a rare sense of peace and deep comfort while in Hawaii. The enormous humpback whales burst out of the sea without warning upon their arrival from their long migration from Alaska. They were a truly thrilling sight. Fiery lava spilled down the mountainside and collided with the chilled ocean with a mighty hiss. We marveled at unspoiled views of The Pacific, tropical waterfalls, lush rainforests, and white volcanic ash high atop the mountains. Visiting the Pearl Harbor Memorial was very emotional for me as it brought back memories of the American soldiers I'd met as a young girl in England and first dreamt of the wonders of America. The wonders of Hawaii are infinite, and I feel blessed for the experience.

Our adventures exposed me to new cultures and expanded my awareness. My worries were softened as I observed countless astounding natural vistas. I renewed my faith in humankind over and over as we met many gracious and altruistic people. Experiencing these exceptional regions in this country made me reconsider my position about spirituality. Perhaps there was a God, and I could believe in the divine. I could have faith in an existence I could not see but could feel.

TRAVEL COMPANIONS

Gloria and Ray became our regular travel companions. After Ray retired as Chief of Police from Upper Dublin, Pennsylvania, he and Gloria moved to South Carolina to escape the chilly northern winters. After many wonderful years living there, they eventually bought a house in nearby Punta Gorda, Florida.

Gloria and I reminisced about our childhood when she and Ray joined us on a trip to England. While there, the four of us went on holiday along the rugged, British coastline and the many quaint villages in Cornwall and Devon. Both Jerry and Ray found it difficult to drive on the left side of the narrow and winding country roads and incessantly harassed one another about their driving skills. Often, these instances of good-natured joking were not so good-natured. During one excursion, Ray abruptly pulled off the cobblestone roadway, hopped out of the car, handed Jerry the keys, and scolded, "You drive and see how much better you can do" Neither of our husbands, it seemed, had much of a sense of humor about their driving skills and Gloria and I laughed at how they carried on like an old married couple. They did not see the humor.

In the tiny ancient village of Polperro in Cornwall, we traveled by horse-drawn buggy through the narrow streets to the legendary King Arthur's castle. Tintagel Castle was in ruins, however we could still see the caves under the cliffs where it had been said Merlin the Magician spent his days. As the sea crashed fiercely against the jagged rock face, I felt a deep, inexplicable connection to this castle and grounds and was reminded of my dear friend Marcia Rock's explanation of reincarnation. I felt as though I had perhaps lived here in a past life.

In 2000, Jerry and I stayed at an ancient bed and breakfast near Ivor's house in Buckinghamshire. As expected, Freda was not going to allow us to visit. Although disappointed, we made the best of my brother's beautiful historic town on our own. We stayed in a charming bed and breakfast cottage. At breakfast one morning, we sat with a smashing group of young teenagers who were delightfully chatty. When we asked them, the group told us they were in Buckinghamshire filming a movie about wizards, witchcraft, and magic. They were shooting scenes in Black Park and shared that in this film it was known as The Forbidden Forest. The young people at the breakfast table promised that, upon the film's release, it would be quite popular. The young actors were engaging and enchanting. They strongly recommended that we go to the movie theater for the 2001 debut. A cheerful and chummy group, the kids chatted about their schooling while shooting a film and how they were enjoying their travels. We said farewell and best of luck to them as we all departed from our breakfast tables.

A year later, the first film of the blockbuster *Harry Potter Series, Harry Potter and the Sorcerer's Stone*, hit the silver screen. We were astounded when we recognized each of the young actors from our lovely exchange at the bed and breakfast. They were spot on; the film turned out to be quite a sensation.

For Cooper's first birthday, I was determined to do something memorable for him. So, during a Bahamas vacation, I watched people parasailing from the sandy beaches. Feeling courageous, I wanted to parasail and capture it on film as a gift so he would see his adventuresome 65-year-old "Nana."

Jerry volunteered to go first. The crew carefully equipped him with a parachute before he briskly ran the length of the platform and jumped onto the boat. As the boat sped away, Jerry lifted off and flew effortlessly into the blue sky. When the boat returned, Jerry landed perfectly to an ovation of cheers all around. He assured me that it was an exhilarating experience and not to feel anxious.

As the crew attached my parachute, I started to panic. Yet, my determination to parasail for my grandson was greater than my fear. Reminding Jerry to snap as many pictures as he could, I darted across the platform and jumped on the boat as instructed. The parachute magically opened. I perched on the bar-type seat, clung to the sidebars, and I rose gently above the water. I looked down at the pure aqua ocean, spotting vibrant tropical fish darting beneath the surface as the island landscape became distant.

As the boat approached the dock, a gust of wind rocked the boat to the left and to the right. Blown off course by the wind, I landed among the waves rather than on the dock. My parachute covered me in the water. Memories of tumbling Bermuda riptides ran through my mind as the crew struggled to untangle me and pull me onto the platform while I gasped for air and shivered frightfully. We returned to the hotel. Anxious to develop the images from the experience, Jerry unintentionally exposed the film, so Cooper never did get to see the evidence of Grandmother's parasailing adventure.

HOME AGAIN

I yearned for a trip home to England to see Ivor. I spoke to Ivor about a visit and he managed to convince Freda to let me stay in their home. I was elated; however, I was concerned she would change her mind upon my arrival. I was happily surprised that both Ivor and Freda embraced me with open arms. Freda was excited to bring me up a steep staircase to the finished attic area of their thatched roof cottage to settle in for the week. The charming attic guest room, I would soon learn, doubled as the room where Ivor and Freda kept their pet rats.

Freda was aware of my intense fear of rats. Nocturnal, the rats scratched and squeaked in their cages all night. By day, Ivor and Freda treated the rats like they would have treated their children, had they children of their own, and allowed the little vermin the run of the cottage. Freda had no pictures of relatives or friends, rather kept framed photos of the rats on all the walls in her home. She gave much of Ivor's hard-earned money to The National Fancy Rat Society and seemed unconcerned that the rats walked on kitchen surfaces and defecated where they pleased. I should have known Freda's welcome was too good to be true.

One evening I was in the kitchen with Ivor while he prepared dinner. Freda emerged from her evening bath and marched into the kitchen wrapped in a bath towel. She opened the oven door, took out food, and threw it in the garbage. She said to me, "Now, look at what you have done. You breathed on our dinner and contaminated it. Now we must start dinner all over again. I told you not to go into the kitchen."

Ivor said nothing and acted as though this was normal behavior. It was difficult to understand whether Freda's behavior was deliberately malicious, or she lacked empathy, but the effect was the same. Freda repelled everyone both from herself and away from my brother. While I was glad to see and spend time with Ivor, I was heartbroken to see the way my brother had been living.

REAL ESTATE

Jerry enjoyed real estate practice on Sanibel Island. He generally purchased properties for himself and rarely sold anything. We bought and renovated several homes hoping to flip and profit. Unfortunately, conditions in the market were not always in our favor.

We bought a gorgeous, castle-like home in Fort Myers and rented it to a single mother and her three children. She seemed like the perfect tenant and her credentials appeared solid. The woman had told us that she had been married to a well-known, English rockstar, but she never shared his name. For a few months, she paid rent regularly. We discovered that she frequently stayed out at night and the children, ages three to fifteen, were left alone. The 13-year-old had Down Syndrome and the oldest child at just fifteen years old was the main caregiver for his siblings. Their dogs were rarely let outside, which led to very unsanitary conditions. The home was uncared for and evolved into a disaster. The neighborhood security guards frequently found her asleep or drunk in her car in the driveway late at night. The tenant finally did vacate the home and we were appalled to discover its condition. Damage to the air-conditioning system would cost $60,000 to repair. In addition, dangerous mold, broken appliances, and the sheer filth of animal waste that permeated the floors and walls made reclamation a losing proposition. In less than a year, the castle home was ruined. Consequently, Jerry believed we had no option than to sell the home at auction to pay the bank.

The timing of the castle home chaos could not have been worse. Having to deal with the difficult tenant and the realization that we would lose a significant investment had put a terrible strain on Jerry both financially and physically. Whether one directly caused the other, we may never know, but during a visit to his doctor, Jerry learned that he had issues with his prostate. After doing a prostate-specific antigen (PSA) blood test, the doctor diagnosed Jerry with prostate cancer. He would need a series of radiation treatments and possibly need surgery.

Jerry's doctors practiced at Lee Memorial Hospital in Fort Myers and Sanibel Causeway traffic was, on a good day, unpredictable. He had a six-week regimen of daily radiation therapy. We decided to sell the canal house on Sanibel Island and bought a condominium in Fort Myers where we, but Jerry in particular, made it our priority to maintain our friendships and our active lifestyle. It may have been just the wisdom of age or maybe even the lack of any other choice considering his financial situation was largely destroyed, but I think it was likely that the cancer diagnosis and the possibility of death nudged Jerry to shift his priorities. He assumed a gentler and more loving outlook toward me and focused more on his relationships. Whatever the reason, I was happy he seemed to be more the man I met in Clifton Park so many years ago.

FAREWELL

Life as we knew it had changed, although we believed that change would only be temporary. Jerry and I absolutely believed that the radiation for the prostate cancer would cure him and that we could resume our routine, if only just from a new home. After all, longevity seemed to run in his family. So, as the radiation treatments continued, we carried on, going to dinner with friends, luncheons, theater, and boating trips. After the six-week regimen was completed, the two of us even traveled to the U.K. to see relatives and to New York to visit Erin and her family. Although Jerry dealt with the physical aftermath of the radiation including exhaustion and, more frequently, excruciating pain from various sources in and on his body, he resolutely marched forward without complaint.

At one point after we had returned to Fort Myers, Jerry's pain became overwhelming, and he was admitted to Lee Memorial Hospital. During one of my daily visits, Jerry and I had a very frank and candid conversation. Jerry explained to me that he recognized that having to watch him in such misery was taking a toll on me. He saw that my health had deteriorated as well. He told me that the pain had become so intense that medication was no longer effective, and he feared that he would never again be able to resume the vibrant quality of life he and we had had. When a nurse entered the room, he asked me to leave the room while he underwent another procedure. I respected his request, walked down the hall, and sat nervously in the waiting room.

Moments later, I was alarmed by an announcement over the loudspeaker, "Elaine Mundt, please return to ICU. Elaine Mundt, please return to the ICU."

When I arrived, a daunting group of nurses, doctors, and police officers met me. The door to Jerry's room was closed and I was not permitted to enter. One of the nurses asked me to sit as the contingent nervously glanced around at everything, but me. I was certain that Jerry had died, and tears welled in my eyes. Despite my very obvious emotional state, no one would tell me anything about what had happened.

A police officer asked if I had anyone I could call to come to the hospital to sit with me. I told them I did and called Gloria and Ray. Once Gloria and Ray arrived, the three of us were led to a private room. The staff had many questions regarding Jerry's state of mind that afternoon. Supported by the presence of my sister, I answered each of the queries.

Finally, as if I were the last person who would have a reason to know, the officer explained the situation. Jerry had entered the tiny bathroom in his room bringing with him his intravenous pole that delivered medications and fluids. Jerry used the IV to create a noose which he tied to the door handle and over the top of the door. Then, he put his neck into the IV tube noose and closed the door where he hung. An orderly had heard sounds from his room and rushed in. When she saw Jerry was not in bed, she attempted to open the bathroom door to no avail. The hospital worker then quickly removed the hinges and found Jerry unconscious. By that time, a team of nurses and doctors converged, placed him on a gurney, and took him to the emergency room.

Jerry's neck was horribly bruised, and he was unable to speak. The IV lines damaged his vocal cords and the purple and red bruises would remain for weeks. Jerry's sunken and emaciated torso was startling. A guard was assigned to Jerry's room and would remain there for several days during which time Jerry was strapped to his bed. He was not permitted to use a phone, computer, or have any contact whatsoever with anyone, outside of the hospital staff and me and other select members of his family, including Erin who had come to help Jerry and to support me. After his physical wounds had healed, Jerry was assigned to a facility where he underwent intense psychological evaluation and rehabilitation. In the meantime, the prostate cancer had surreptitiously advanced at an alarming rate.

Once he was thought to be mentally stable, Jerry was released. Upon his arrival home, Jerry's urologist taught me to administer the tube insertion for the urostomy pouch. I learned the procedure to save Jerry the agony of going to the hospital each time the pouch needed changing. He sincerely thanked me for my care as the two of us joked about my new nursing abilities. Jerry gave me a name tag that said, "Nurse Ratchet" and, although he was still in agony, his spirits seemed to have been lifted.

A guarded optimism for recovery, however, transformed to dread as Jerry's oncologist discovered the prostate cancer had progressed. Jerry urged the urologist to perform a urinary diversion surgery and remove his prostate, although the urologist strongly disagreed. Because the radiation treatments had created very fragile tissue surrounding the cancer, the doctor did not believe he could not safely operate without damaging Jerry's bladder. There was also a high risk of infection that could prove to be septic.

It was only reasonable to seek a second opinion, so the two of us traveled to the Mayo Clinic in Minneapolis. After a battery of testing, The Mayo Clinic recommended proceeding with the prostate surgery. So, upon our return to Fort Myers, Jerry insisted that his urologist proceed with the risky urinary diversion surgery. It was an outpatient procedure and would result in urine excretion from the side of his stomach for the rest of his life. By this time Jerry was in so much pain that a lifetime urinary inconvenience was a small price to pay. As he had already demonstrated, there was really nothing that Jerry was not willing to endure to escape the pain he experienced. So, when we returned from Minneapolis, we scheduled the surgery. We made plans to get takeout after the outpatient surgery and bid the cancer, "Farewell."

Jerry's procedure was scheduled to take two hours. By the time I had waited five, stressful hours the surgeon finally emerged to tell me about the surgery. I didn't notice at first that he was in tears. He hugged me and explained to me that there had been an issue. An ambulance would take Jerry to the ICU again at Lee Memorial and suggested that I follow it there.

During the surgery, the surgeon had inadvertently damaged Jerry's bladder, which was one of the reasons the urologist was reluctant to perform the procedure. A small laceration of the bladder caused bleeding in places where the body was not supposed to bleed. Shortly thereafter, Jerry contracted sepsis and MRSA and his condition deteriorated quickly. He lost consciousness and was transferred from ICU to hospice.

After having lost consciousness because of the unsuccessful urinary diversion, Jerry never woke. Surrounded by his children, Scott and JoAnn, Ray and Gloria, my Scott and Erin, and me, Jerry passed peacefully.

Months later, I held a beautiful celebration of life ceremony for Jerry at Lighthouse Beach on Sanibel Island. Along with our family and friends, a huge group from the Sanibel Power Squadron came dressed in sharp, white uniforms. Later, as our condo was filled with friends and family, I asked that they not shed tears and all obliged. I wanted to hear inspiring stories about Jerry and honor his memory and life. One of the Power Squadron men with the most beautiful voice sang a tender lullaby to me in the kitchen. Every guest there listened in awe. It was a beautifully touching moment that left me speechless and in tears. We sailed into the majestic Gulf of Mexico off Sanibel Island and gently sprinkled Jerry's remains into the salty waves that he loved dearly.

A financial catastrophe unfolded upon Jerry's death. I was unaware of many of the financial issues that Jerry had created. He had invested in properties including a condominium, three homes, and four timeshare properties which were heavily mortgaged and needed to be liquidated immediately. Mortgage payments, taxes, and homeowner association fees, attorney fees, were due.

Managing grief and financial implosion, I was overwhelmed by depression. I was intent on being proactive before the darkness of that depression engulfed me. I decided to take a trip to England alone. I wanted to fulfill the promise I had made to both my father and Uncle Syd by sprinkling their ashes on my grandfather's grave. There were ailing family members and friends that I visited, fully aware that it would be the last time in their presence. The trip was worth this alone. I felt a sense of peace. Upon my return to the states, I moved to New York to be close to Erin and my grandchildren, Cooper and Sawyer.

SALT IN THE WOUND

There clearly comes a time in everyone's life when the fulcrum on the scale of life's milestones tilt from engagements, marriages, and births to profound disappointments, diagnoses of life-threatening illness, and the loss of loved ones.

Four months after Jerry's passing, I learned of heart-wrenching news from California that my beloved baby brother, Brian faced late-stage esophageal cancer and there were no treatment options. At that point, Brian's only option was palliative care. I flew to Brian's Upland, California home to offer loving support. Brian's children and I cared for him at his home as we endeavored to create a state of comfort and positivity to make his final days in this life more beautiful. We managed to tell stories and even joke at times to lighten all our spirits, but cancer does not have a sense of humor. Brian died in my arms within the week.

At 80-years old, Freda succumbed to cancer herself. Since I had not been able to have much of a relationship with my brother Ivor because Freda had, at best, made it difficult and, at worst, forbade it, I did not know much about Freda's illness. After her death, however, Ivor began to meet his longtime neighbors who previously did not dare approach him as a result of Freda's eccentricities. As a widower, however, Ivor created an entirely new social life and built friendships that had previously been out of his reach. Ivor also resolved to visit family, including his sisters in the United States. Gloria and I were overjoyed and enjoyed rich and wonderful visits with our older brother while Ivor bonded his nieces and nephews.

Unfortunately, during one of his visits, Ivor took a terrible fall and broke his hip. He had surgery and rehabilitation. He eventually traveled back to England with a nurse escort. It was difficult for Ivor to return to an empty home and even more difficult for me to see him leave. We communicated often on Facetime, which made the separation bearable. Although I was comforted seeing him on the screen on one hand, I noticed Ivor's health deteriorated during a relatively short period of time. He finally managed a visit to the doctor and he, too, learned he had cancer. In 2018, Ivor entered the hospital with late-stage esophageal cancer, like our younger brother, Brian. Erin and her cousin, Sean, flew to England to comfort Ivor and to help arrange his affairs. The three chatted and laughed over old memories and they remained by his hospital bedside until he could breathe no more. Ivor was 87-years old and truly died in character with a smile on his face. Ivor's dying words were, "I will at last join the love of my life."

I hope that he did.

Perhaps hastened by the stress and distraction of my grief and financial woes, I encountered a series of health crises myself. Some of these issues were a result of unfortunate circumstances, while others were health related and conceivably precipitated my mental state. First among them was an incident when Erin's lovely Labrador puppy, Jett, enthusiastically greeted me with a fond, leaping hello and caused me to fall on the deck and fracture my hip. Cooper called an ambulance. An emergency hip replacement surgery and a miserable stay in a rehabilitation facility followed. A year later, on New Year's Eve, Erin brought me to the emergency room as I was experiencing severe chest pains. Doctors discovered three pulmonary emboli in my lungs as well as a recurrence of breast cancer. I remained in the hospital for another ten days and was prescribed blood thinners to alleviate the clots at Orange Regional Medical Center (ORMC) in Middletown, New York.

Upon my release, Erin picked me up to take me home after the treatment to dissolve the pulmonary emboli. At the hospital where I had just been released, a man wielded a knife and threatened to kill patients and doctors alike. New York State Troopers were en route to the hospital to deal with the crisis. A rookie New York State Trooper sped irresponsibly on Crystal Run Road near the ORMC without using sirens or flashing lights, sped through the intersection against a red light where we were turning left. The Trooper crashed his cruiser violently directly into the passenger's side door of Erin's car. The car spun in three complete rotations, airbags dropping all around us as Erin and I locked eyes. Suddenly, the car came to a halt. Several of Erin's ribs were broken and I sustained deep tissue hematomas and a severe injury to my knee, but we survived. We were driven by ambulance right back into the hospital we had left minutes earlier.

GEICO Insurance paid the claim to replace Erin's car, paid for the hospital bills and paid for the totaled police vehicle because the collision was so clearly the fault of the New York State Police Trooper who hit Erin's car. GEICO and Erin's attorney advised us that suing the New York State Police would be fruitless. We would end up spending a great deal of money and gain nothing from our efforts. Erin received no citation for the accident and, to my knowledge, the New York State Trooper who caused the accident was not reprimanded and was able to keep his job.

After the accident with the New York State Trooper, I was admitted again at ORMC, but was released a couple of days later. This time, I made it back home without further incident.

After much consideration, my unilateral mastectomy was performed a few months later at Good Samaritan Hospital in Suffern, New York. My hip replacement was still very painful, and my knee was still swollen and bruised as a result of the accident with New York State Trooper. The surgery was successful, for the most part, but on one occasion when I tried to get out of bed to use the bathroom, I fell. This time I could not blame Jett. I hit my head which caused a delusional state in which I hallucinated that my English relatives and friends, including my mother, father, Brian, my cousin Gerald, all of whom had passed away, were in the waiting room and were hungry, and that Erin would not let them see me. In my confused state, I relentlessly called Erin and begged her to let them see me. I wanted her to bring cucumber sandwiches so we could all feast. I was angry with Erin and could not understand why she had come alone to visit me.

Erin met with a team of physicians and psychologists. I was unstable and they paired me with another delusional person in the psych ward, where I did not realize that I was a patient. My roommate was also round the bend, so to speak, and kept yelling for her husband. I told my equally delusional roommate, "Sorry, your husband is dead and is not coming to see you." I convinced her he had passed away. Her husband was, in fact, alive and he was in the waiting room, right next door. For my efforts, the doctors gave me a private room. I could not go home as I was experiencing many peculiar hallucinations. I was sent by ambulance to a rehabilitation facility to convalesce from surgery and my psychological condition. Eventually, I recovered and went to live with my daughter.

Again in 2018 when I was alone in the house, I fell down a flight of deck stairs at Erin's home. I waited on the ground for close to an hour before Sawyer discovered me and called for an ambulance. This time, I broke my clavicle and six ribs and spent three more months in rehabilitation at Valley View in Goshen, N.Y. When I recovered from this setback, I thought it best to move from Erin's house. For many reasons, not the least of which were the numerous stairs and the loveable, but sometimes unpredictable dogs, I took an apartment in a senior living community in the same town where I could live independently in an apartment community designed with safety and quality of life for older residents in mind. Considering I was able to see Erin, my grandchildren, and the friends I had made locally, my new living arrangement was the perfect situation.

During the wee hours on a cold winter night in February 2020 just as COVID-19 had begun to enter our vocabulary, I began hemorrhaging from my nose. I managed to get to the phone after a few hours and I called Erin for help. She phoned for an ambulance and rushed over immediately. When she arrived, my apartment looked like a violent crime scene with blood trailing from my sheets to the rug and throughout the bathroom. Paramedics loaded me into the ambulance and drove me to the emergency room. I was admitted into the hospital and stayed in the ICU for weeks. Once again, I suffered from hallucinations. Patients were completely isolated, and no visitors were allowed due to COVID-19 restrictions. This made for a difficult and frightening recovery.

Doctors were never able to determine the cause of the hemorrhage, but one thing was clear; I could no longer live independently as my strength was fading and it was not safe to drive a car. I had no more strength than that of a kitten and I needed assistance with the small things and the big things a person is required to do every day. My family and I agreed that the place for me would be an assisted living facility where I will probably live the rest of my days.

I do my best at keeping a positive attitude and focus on all that is good. I am grateful for the time with Erin and my grandsons who I usually see several times a week. Erin visits me or takes me to her house or to get lunch in town. Often, Cooper or Sawyer join us. It is healing seeing their gorgeous faces.

I enjoy comforting the elderly residents. When they have trouble communicating, I listen and become their voice. Some need a laugh or a smile, I provide it joyfully. Others need a hand when their undergarments are failing them, and I've had that problem my whole life so I know exactly what to do. My body tells me I am old, but my mind says otherwise, and for this I am grateful. I will do until I can do no more.

NY State Senator Martin M. Solomon and Elaine at the State Senate, Albany, NY, 1980.

Wedding Day with Jerry, Chicago, 1983.

Miss Adventure and Erin in Bailey's Harbor,
Door County Wisconsin, 1995.

Erin's home in Santa Fe, New Mexico, 1998.

Ivor and Elaine on a swing in Warwick, NY, 2016

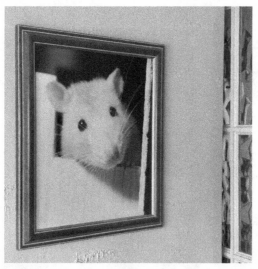

Pet rat photo at Ivor's Buckinghamshire
cottage, 2018

Ivor before his passing, 2018.

Erin and Elaine at Erin and Tom's wedding party, 2021.

My grandson, Cooper at Mattingly's Tavern in Florida, NY, 2022.

My grandson, Sawyer, 2022.

Scott and Elaine at Mattingly's Tavern, in Florida, NY, 2022.

Erin and Tom at a local concert on Railroad GreenWarwick, NY, 2022.

EPILOGUE

If you, my reader, are wondering at this point whether I am writing my own epilogue, I am. My story may be coming to an end, but I am still writing it.

I had lost touch with Prince Ungku Nazaruddin bin Ungku Muda Muhammad, the man known to me as, "Ruddin," after he returned to Malaysia. I researched him for this memoir, was able to find precious little information about him save a few photos, vague references to his military service, and a bit of biographical information. One reference reported that Ruddin rose to the rank of General in the Malayan (Malaysian) Armed Forces and another suggested he took part in a military operation in The Congo in the late 1960's. Apparently, Ruddin did marry a second time after he divorced his first wife, his cousin. Apparently, that marriage had truly been a marriage to prevent his cousin from becoming a rest house girl for the Japanese soldiers. Ruddin had nine children. He passed away on December 2, 2004, at the age of 81.

Ron Tarwater is still married to Carol, to whom I still affectionately refer as "WhatsHerName." Ron and Carol have lived in Saratoga Springs, New York for the past six years. I only occasionally speak with Ron. Scott and Erin give me news about him when there is any news to give. Ron's health seems to be pretty good and still gets around well for a man who will be 90-years-old in 2024.

Sadly, we lost Ray from complications related to Alzheimer's disease in 2015. My little sister Gloria lives in a lovely senior living community in Lititz, Pennsylvania near her oldest son, Bob and his wife, Karen. Between Bob, her second son, Tom, and her daughter Lisa, Gloria has nine grandchildren and four great-grandchildren. Gloria, too, is in good health and I speak with her regularly and have also gotten to see her once or twice a year during the past few years.

Scott lives in Missouri City, Texas outside of Houson, and has been the Corporate Director of Wine & Special Events at Landry's Restaurants where he has worked for the past 21-years. Scott married, but perhaps because of the rigors of his career, divorced and has no children. Scott travels a great deal opening new restaurant locations for Landry's all over the world. His home is on a golf course, and he has become quite a good golfer. He makes a point of visiting New York two or three times a year to visit both Ron and me. I enjoy those visits from Scott, and we always have a lot of fun.

After a 20-year marriage, Erin divorced and subsequently fell in love with Tom Mattingly. In Tom, who is originally from Missouri like her father, Erin found her soulmate. I have never seen my daughter happier. Erin and Tom are two creative souls who complement each other in many ways. They opened a local tavern nearby and work together daily and have created a wonderful business. Erin moved into Tom's Civil War Era Victorian home. I relish the days, now, that I sit in front of the warm fireplace in their home sipping my tea as their King Charles Cavalier Spaniel lays alongside me.

Charles III's coronation as the King of England was the first in almost nine decades I did not personally witness. Edward VIII and Wallis Simpson have been replaced with Prince Harry and Meghan Markle, Winston Churchill with Rishi Sunak, Adolph Hitler with Vladmir Putin, Franklin Roosevelt with Joe Biden, and me wearing a bonnet, being pushed in a pram with me pushing a walker.

With the perspective of the experiences a long life, I know how much the world has changed and, also, how little the world has changed. The world turned before me, and it will continue to turn when I am no longer here. During the time I am here however, I and each of us have a choice to make every moment of every day. We can choose to make that world a better place, if even by a little, or not. When faced with one of those moments, I hope you choose to make the world a little better.

Gumbeaux and Elaine at Erin and Tom's home in Warwick, NY, 2023.